ALLAN DIB

LEAN
MARKETING

More leads. More profit.
Less marketing.

PAGE TWO

ISBN 978-1-77458-394-4 (hardcover)
ISBN 978-1-77458-395-1 (ebook)

Published by Page Two

Edited by Scott Steedman and Shannon Clark
Copyedited by David Marsh
Proofread by Alison Strobel
Jacket, interior design, and illustrations by Fiona Lee
Printed and bound in Canada
Distributed in Canada by Raincoast Books
Distributed in the US and internationally by Macmillan

24 25 26 27 28   5 4 3 2 1

LeanMarketing.com

To Sarah-Jane,
Thanks for filling every day with
your love, kindness, and softness.

To my peeps gone too soon:

Dad, I miss you each and every day.

Maia, you were a second mother to me.
Thanks for always believing in me and cheering me on.

Reza, thanks for all the laughs,
schemes, and friendship.

Contents

FORCE MULTIPLIER 3: PROCESSES *191*

Introduction

Let Your Light Shine

Discovering the best-kept secret is awesome. Being the best-kept secret is soul-crushing. Timeless wisdom tells us:

> A city set on a hill cannot be hidden. Nor do people light a lamp and put it under a basket, but on a stand, and it gives light to all in the house. In the same way, let your light shine before others, so that they may see your good works.

But how do you "set your city on a hill" so that your audience knows you exist? How do you get "your light to shine before others" so that they're attracted to you? How do you get them to desire and value "the good works" that you have to offer? That's the essence of this book. I'll share the exact framework my clients and I use to attract, convert, and retain customers every day.

I suspect the products or services you offer could help many people. Your "good works" deserve visibility, attention, and momentum. However, as you and I know, there's a world of difference between deserving success and actually attaining it. If merit alone led to business success, we could stop the book right here and save us both a lot of time and energy.

The reality is you don't get what you deserve; you get what you negotiate. If life were a meritocracy, then nurses, firefighters, and schoolteachers would be the highest-paid people in our society. Yet many entrepreneurs still hope that the value they bring will shine through in the marketplace.

Hope is not an effective marketing strategy.

Value needs to be elevated and made visible.

When merit and visibility combine, they create an unstoppable force.

Is This You?

Do any of the following scenarios feel familiar?

- You incinerated huge sums of money on a marketing or branding agency, and all you had to show for it was a shiny new logo and some pretty design. Impact on your revenue: approximately zero.

- You hired a website developer, only to have the project take longer and cost more in time, money, or energy than you ever imagined, yet it still isn't generating leads.

- You were encouraged by some consultant, "guru," or copywriter to do marketing that feels pushy, cheesy, or sleazy—marketing that you're not proud of and would make you cringe if you showed it to friends, family, or colleagues.

- You hired someone to run your marketing and were underwhelmed with their results.

- You flushed piles of money down the toilet on ads that attracted low-quality leads.

It's not that any of these initiatives or the people involved were bad. Marketing and branding agencies are awesome. Web developers are unsung heroes. Copywriters are worth their weight in gold. Heads of marketing are rock stars. Digital ad propeller-heads are virtuosos.

The problem was that you set them up for failure. They know how to do branding, websites, copy, and digital ads, but you expected them to be the messiah who would solve all your marketing problems. They sold and delivered a tool or tactic, but you didn't have the right infrastructure to plug these into. You may not even have an infrastructure at all and just be doing random acts of marketing.

If you're a head of marketing or a marketing consultant, you're not off the hook either. After all, running marketing is your job. At some stage, you'll want a pay raise, higher fees, or career progression. Wouldn't it be great if getting these things was a no-brainer? Your boss or your client *wants* to pay you more, but they need to see a return on their investment in you. You need to be a profit center, not an expense. Nothing freaks out an entrepreneur, at least a sane one, more than increasing expenses while revenue flatlines or declines.

Throughout this book, I'll use the term "entrepreneur." My definition of an entrepreneur is someone who solves problems for a profit. You could be a founder, business owner, head of marketing, business leader, CEO, or anyone with a hand in getting more prospects, leads, customers, and ultimately revenue into your organization. You may be at a startup, at a business that's already doing well and wanting to scale up, or at a mature enterprise.

I'll also make frequent references to "customers." Depending on your industry or line of business, you may refer to your "customers" as clients, patients, users, donors, members, or some other designation. Regardless, the principles are the same—the goal is to attract, convert, and retain them.

Don't Be a Midwit

Can you accept conflicting ideas without your head exploding? I hope so; otherwise, you're probably not going to enjoy this book.

Have you ever seen the midwit meme? It's an intelligence bell curve. At the low end is a Quasimodo-like numbskull with a low IQ, at the opposite end is a Jedi-like genius with a super-high IQ, and in the middle is the midwit. There are variations of the meme, but usually both numbskull and genius reach the same simple conclusion. The numbskull reaches it because he's too dumb to overthink things, the genius because he's wise and values simplicity. Meanwhile, the midwit's brain is close to exploding with analysis, arguments, and rebuttals. He ends up with an answer that sounds intelligent but is wrong or unproductive.

Both numbskulls and geniuses are usually open to new ideas. However, the midwit loves pointing out the contradictions and why something won't work or is wrong.

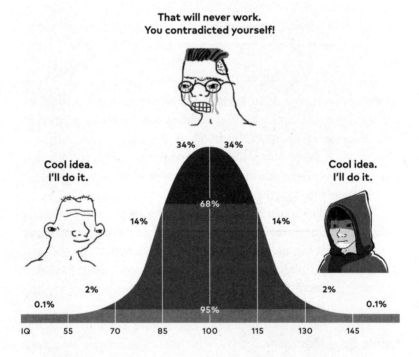

It's human nature to like our own version of reality, and we don't like it being messed with. We enjoy being with people who agree with us. We enjoy reading, watching, or listening to things that agree with our worldview. When someone challenges our version of reality, we find all sorts of ways and reasons to reject them.

The world is complicated, nuanced, and often contradictory, with multiple ways of being right or wrong. The midwits are hell-bent on being right. At times when I was being a midwit, one of my early business mentors would ask, "Allan, would you rather be right or rich?" Midwits want to be right. Be a numbskull or be a genius, but don't waste your life being a midwit.

There's no profit in trying to figure out why something won't work for you, why it's contradictory, or why it can't be done. Work on figuring out *how* it could work for you.

Can you hold multiple conflicting ideas in your mind? Let's see...

Marketing Is Easy

Hustle culture glorifies "the grind." While I've never shied away from hard work, I also never understood this martyr complex. Your work or business will make up a large part of your life. It should be fun, not a grind. The only type of grinding that's actually fun is very much outside the scope of this book.

Instead of the grind, I encourage you to build a business that you'll love—one that's profitable. One where you look forward to Mondays instead of dreading them.

For this to become a reality, you'll need a solid grasp of how to reliably get leads, customers, and ultimately profit in the door. If you master marketing, you can make a lot of mistakes and still win big. Marketing covers a multitude of sins.

The good news is marketing is easy.

Easy means it's simple, not that it's no effort. Easy means that anybody can do it, and you don't need to be a genius with the amazing idea that beats all the competitors. Easy means you'll get consistent results if you follow a proven framework and process.

Marketing is a skill, and like any skill, it can be learned. My work is helping people and organizations develop or enhance their marketing capabilities. One of the most satisfying parts of what I do is seeing the breakthroughs resulting from mastering this skill. Everything changes. Startups gain traction, businesses that had hit growth plateaus smash through them, and already very success-ful companies reach even higher levels of success. If any of these things sound similar to your goals, then you're in the right place.

However, breakthroughs require you to break things...

Marketing Is Hard

I'm going to level with you. Marketing is really hard. Most people who half-heartedly "try it" won't get any results at all. (Kind of like most people who buy gym equipment won't ever look like the people in the gym equipment commercial.) After a short time, they'll throw their arms up in the air and exclaim, "I've tried everything!"

I hate to be the bearer of bad news, but there's no magic bullet or easy button. So what's it going to be like?

If you commit to the work and actually *implement* the stuff in this book, it'll often feel like crawling on your hands and knees, butt naked, over broken glass. You'll go through various stages of frustration, disappointment, and anger. If you can make it through that, you'll eventually get to the light at the end of the cold, dark tunnel. You'll have developed the single most valuable business skill—the ability to attract, convert, and retain ideal customers.

I estimate that only 3 percent of people are real action-takers who'll tolerate the pain. Will you be one of them?

Pride and Prejudice

How did you do with our first conflicting idea? If you haven't thrown this book across the room in a fit of anger, then things are looking good so far. (There'll be plenty of opportunities for that as we go.) Let's try another couple of conflicting ideas.

There are many different approaches to marketing, and it's seductive to look for "the one right way," but that's the domain of the midwit. There's value in taking in diverse perspectives and using the best ideas from each. Some of my best insights have come from people I generally didn't agree with.

Let's look at some of the different perspectives in the marketing space.

At one end of the spectrum, there's Seth Godin, who advocates creating something remarkable for your tribe of true believers and letting them spread the word.

Seth's message is very attractive to creative types: artists, writers, and freelancers who are repulsed by modern marketing, which they perceive as sleazy. To be fair, their biases are not unfounded. Seth gives them the permission they crave to focus on their craft and the encouragement they need to ship their work and share their talents with the world. He cheers them on to change the culture.

(Of course, this is highly reductionist. You can't summarize a man's life work in a few paragraphs and do him justice. I respect Seth, and you'll undoubtedly see his influence on my work. I encourage you to read his books, listen to him speak, and attend his workshops to get a deeper and more nuanced understanding of his message.)

At the other end of the spectrum, there's Dan Kennedy, whose roots are in the world of mail order, infomercials, and direct response marketing. He emphasizes measurable results above all else. His brash, no-nonsense approach encourages sending highly targeted offers using emotionally charged copy, with urgency and strong guarantees. He's outspoken about his disdain for brand marketing. Dan has an intense prejudice against any marketing activity that doesn't elicit an action and have measurable results.

Dan's message is attractive to information marketers, brick-and-mortar businesses, and practitioners delivering tangible transformations in healthcare, financial services, and education. Many of the techniques used by so-called Internet marketers originate with Dan and his predecessors like Claude Hopkins, John Caples, and Robert Collier. Again, you'll see the influence of Dan and other direct response marketers in my work also.

If you study direct response marketing, you'll learn more about human psychology (and how to exploit it for profit) than you'll ever learn from a college degree in business and psychology combined. In direct response marketing, constant visibility and contact with the target audience are paramount.

(A few years ago, Dan was gravely ill. Despite being in a hospice bed in what was believed to be his final few days, he still wrote a series of sales letters to his customers. Fortunately, Dan recovered—but that's a hardcore commitment to the craft if I've ever seen one.)

We can learn a lot from both approaches. I suggest using identity labels carefully and sparingly. The more labels and isms you apply to yourself, the stupider you get. That's why I don't identify as a "brand guy" or "direct response guy." For now, I'm sticking to "marketer."

Even identifying as a marketer feels like what I imagine it's like admitting to being a sex worker. While virtually everyone wants what you do, they simultaneously look down on you and judge you for it. This distaste for us marketers is perhaps somewhat deserved.

I love the results-driven approach of direct response marketing. But I'd be lying if I didn't admit to being a bit embarrassed by the sleazy feel that has often characterized it: gaudy design, big red headlines in ugly fonts, huge "buy now" buttons, outlandish claims, and fake scarcity.

I also love the idea of meticulously crafting remarkable work that I'm proud to share with the world. But the stereotypical image of a starving artist living in obscurity feels equally embarrassing.

Could we take the ruthless street smarts of direct response marketing and still build something we're intensely proud of? Something we wouldn't hesitate to show friends and family?

Could we build a strong brand on the back of solid, measurable results instead of the creative indulgence and wastefulness typical of brand marketing?

These are conflicting ideas. The midwits are already crafting clever rebuttals to prove why this would never work.

I'd encourage you to be either the numbskull or the genius and hold these conflicting ideas in mind as you figure out how to make them work for you.

FOUNDATIONS

1

Leaning Into Marketing

CHAPTER 1 SUMMARY

Much of marketing has become bloated, ineffective, and wasteful. A lean approach to marketing helps you build goodwill and brand equity while also driving a strong return on investment.

Highlights covered in this chapter include:

- The origin of lean marketing

- How the lean movement transformed Japanese manufacturing from the worst in the world to the best and how it's now transforming marketing

- Why marketing must become a value-creating activity

- The importance of embedding marketing throughout the entire product life cycle and customer journey

- The contrast between brand marketing and direct response marketing and how lean marketing blends the best of each

- The importance of product-market fit in ensuring your marketing is successful

- The three force multipliers that will dramatically amplify your marketing results

How Marketing Got Lean

"What the fuck am I doing here?" I thought to myself, sitting in the back of the car as we drove through the streets of León. This was my last major stop on an intense, five-week speaking tour across North America. I was hot, uncomfortable, and mentally and physically exhausted. I missed my family, my home, and my dog. My only comfort was that I'd be sharing a stage the next day with Guy Kawasaki and Salim Ismail. I figured if they thought this event was worth traveling to, then it was probably worth my time too.

León is a city in the central Mexican state of Guanajuato that has become a global automotive manufacturing hub. The conference was put on by the state and the automotive industry. The place was teeming with people who'd reaped enormous benefits from lean manufacturing and was a very appropriate catalyst for what would later become known as lean marketing.

When the mind feels weak, logic often falls by the wayside, allowing anxious thoughts to dominate. The driver sent to pick me up from the airport was armed. Seeing that I'd noticed his gun, he joked that it was unlikely he'd need to use it. Uncharacteristically, I was in no mood for jokes.

At the time, there had been a lot of negative press and politicking about Mexico and crime. And my having recently binge-watched *Breaking Bad* didn't help. When the car pulled up at a red light, I imagined us getting stopped by gang members from a drug cartel brandishing weapons and shouting at us to get out. I pictured myself taking cover behind the car as my driver and the gangsters exchanged gunfire. A bullet pierces the body of the car and lodges deep in my chest. I fall to the ground, gasping for air. My hand smears blood on the car window as I struggle to get back up, but it's no use. I slump to the ground, ending my short journey in a place I had no business being.

Of course, none of that happened. My armed driver and I arrived at the hotel without incident. I was warmly welcomed and treated like royalty. The hand towel in the bathroom even had my name stitched on it.

As is often the case in life, low points in the moment become turning points in retrospect. What I thought of as the final obligation on my tour became the highlight. The hospitality and friendliness of the Mexican people overwhelmed me.

The party the night before the event was one of the most incredible I'd ever been to. A robotic arm that looked like it was from a car factory served wine while a full orchestra pumped out hit after hit. There was some novelty or entertainment in every corner.

When I was scheduled to speak the next day, it felt like I'd stepped into some alternate reality. Long lines of attendees waited for me to sign their books and take a photo with me. Didn't these people realize I was a nobody? I couldn't go to the bathroom without being stopped and asked for a photo or autograph. As I walked around the venue, I heard people whisper, "That's Allan Dib." It felt like I was the subject of an elaborate prank. To this day, I can't account for my celebrity at that event, but it was certainly fun. "I'm a big deal in Mexico" is a running joke I use with my team whenever I need to pull rank.

At this event, I met Luis Socconini, a friendly, mild-mannered fellow who expressed how much he'd enjoyed my book. When I asked what business he was in, he explained that he was a founder of the Lean Six Sigma Institute and the author of several books on Lean Six Sigma. "You know, I consider your book to be lean marketing," he added. This was the first time I'd heard the term. Although I didn't think much of it at the time, it was a turning point in how I thought about the work I was doing to simplify marketing. We chatted for a while, exchanged pleasantries, and promised to keep in touch. Luis later became a client and a friend.

His gift was helping me see the intersection between the lean movement and the work I was doing in marketing. This led me to define the nine principles of lean marketing that I share with you throughout this book, as well as their practical implementation.

From Lean Manufacturing to Lean Marketing

Lean is a methodology pioneered in the world of manufacturing. It focuses on eliminating waste and increasing efficiency.

Because of the direct correlation with profitability, many manufacturers have adopted or converted to lean. A pioneer in this space is Toyota, who, in the 1950s and 1960s, developed the Toyota Production System, a precursor to lean manufacturing.

It's hard to overstate the importance of the lean manufacturing movement. After the Second World War ended, Japan was in a very bad state—its major cities were devastated, its resources were drained, and its industries were broken. At the time, mass production, which originated with the Ford Motor Company, was the dominant manufacturing method. This style of manufacturing produces large quantities of identical products and is epitomized in Henry Ford's famous quote, "You can have any color as long as it's black." Mass manufacturing requires high inventory levels, huge, specialized machines, and large investments in raw materials, infrastructure, and energy. This was simply not an option for war-torn Japanese manufacturers. They needed a different way to gain a competitive advantage.

Fast-forward to the 1970s and 1980s. Japan had become a global manufacturing powerhouse known for its high-quality, reliable products, particularly in electronics, automobiles, and machinery. Brands like Toyota, Honda, Sony, and Canon had gained worldwide recognition and respect. The Japanese manufacturing approach has since been widely studied and emulated by companies all over the world.

"Made in Japan" went from being a joke to being synonymous with excellence. This transformation is illustrated in the movie *Back to the Future Part III* when Doc (from the 1950s) says, "No wonder this circuit failed—it says 'Made in Japan,'" to which Marty (from the 1980s) replies, "What do you mean, Doc? All the best stuff is made in Japan." On the back of lean manufacturing, Japan became the second-largest economy in the world. To this day, if you want a reliable, durable, and low-cost car, it's hard to go past a Toyota.

Outside of manufacturing, lean thinking has been applied to industries like healthcare, software development, and service industries. Lean methodologies are deeply integrated into some of the world's most valuable companies.

Jeff Bezos frequently cites *Lean Thinking* as one of his favorite business books.

In it, authors James Womack and Daniel Jones define lean as "a way to do more and more with less and less—less human effort, less equipment, less time, and less space—while coming closer and closer to providing customers with exactly what they want."

Some key principles include defining value from the customer's viewpoint and delivering it, continuous improvement in how value is delivered, eliminating the use of resources that are wasteful or don't contribute value, and producing what's needed only when it's needed. The goal is to eliminate all waste in the value delivery process.

Many lean concepts are highly applicable to the marketing world. In lean, waste is defined as anything that consumes resources the customer doesn't value.

There's enormous waste in mass marketing. It focuses on interrupting as many people as possible with a standard message about an average product. This is wasteful, inefficient, and provides no value for the vast majority of people who it interrupts.

Your marketing should be so valuable that your target market would pay you to receive it. While you may price it at no cost, there should be a genuine potential to turn it into a paid product in its own right.

LEAN MARKETING PRINCIPLE 1:
Create value for your target market with your marketing

A way to think about this is to consider the externalities your marketing creates. An externality is the side effect of an economic activity that impacts others. Most externalities are negative, like air pollution caused by a factory, which harms the health of nearby residents.

A positive externality brings a benefit that wasn't paid for by the beneficiary; for example, if your neighbor plants and maintains a beautiful garden that elevates your neighborhood and that you enjoy when you look out your window.

Most marketing creates negative externalities. It's self-focused, interruption-based, and irrelevant to most who see it. It's spewing pollution, just like the thick smoke from the smokestack of a factory. Lean marketing is the opposite—it creates positive externalities, benefiting even those who'll never become customers.

Another common area of waste is when marketing operates in a silo—when it's engaged after the fact and tasked with peddling whatever product or service has been developed. This is lipstick on a pig.

You'll notice much of what we cover in this book is outside the scope of what would traditionally be considered "marketing." I discuss things like onboarding, customer retention, referrals, building a team, and much more. Why would we do that in a marketing book?

We do this because marketing is happening throughout your entire organization. It's happening in your sales conversations, it's happening in your delivery process, it's happening in your customer service. You may or may not call it marketing, but these interactions with current and prospective customers affect future buying decisions, customer lifetime value, and revenue.

By being intentional and integrating marketing throughout your organization, you make your marketing activities far more effective. If your customer service team recognized opportunities to upsell or bundle additional products, wouldn't that increase your customer lifetime value? If your sales team was genuinely helpful and prospects looked forward to speaking with them, wouldn't that increase your conversion rates? If your customer onboarding process was smooth, wouldn't that reduce churn?

Two important concepts in lean are *value stream mapping* and *flow*. Value stream mapping involves identifying and mapping every step of a product's or service's life cycle: from raw materials through production of the product or service, customer delivery, customer use, and final disposal. Doing this can identify steps that add value and those that do not.

Flow ensures that value-adding activities move smoothly throughout. This is often achieved by reducing batch sizes, leveling out workloads, and eliminating bottlenecks. Separate departments are disbanded and merged into a single unified team for each product line. Seeing marketing as part of your value proposition means that you can move to a flow-based approach. Marketing gets integrated into your entire organization.

The mass approach is to have everyone siloed in their own department. This is what happens in most companies. The product development or design team comes up with a concept, the engineering team then makes a prototype, the manufacturing team produces the end product, and finally, it falls to the marketing team to figure out how to sell this stuff and to whom. Often, it's there that everyone finds out there isn't a strong demand for the product, or it doesn't really address a problem that the customer is willing to pay for. The perceived efficiency of separate, specialized departments created the ultimate business inefficiency—wasted resources and missed opportunities.

The classic bickering between sales and marketing departments is a typical symptom of this. The sales team complains that the leads suck, and the marketing team complains that the sales team can't close. And what's the point of awesome marketing and sales, anyway, when your delivery team creates a leaky bucket by frustrating and losing customers?

The lean approach is to have marketing embedded throughout. It needs to be baked into the product. Otherwise, you end up with a lot of waste: crappy leads that aren't a good fit, a sales team pushing hard and price-discounting to close, and customer service that's constantly putting out fires.

LEAN MARKETING PRINCIPLE 2:

Embed marketing throughout the entire product life cycle and customer journey

A central question in lean is, Which of our activities are value-creating and which are inefficient or wasteful? Your goal is to create customers as efficiently as possible.

This doesn't mean a cold, transactional view of customers. Far from it. As you'll see throughout this book, creating goodwill, customer satisfaction, and a happy team are central to what we do as marketers and business leaders. Not for some fuzzy, feel-good reason but because it's good business. It's an efficient way to build a business and multiply customers and revenue.

Lean marketing is a systematic approach to making this happen. You define and deliver value to customers and prospects based on *their* viewpoint. You build goodwill and brand equity in the customer creation process. You create value for your audience and drive measurable results.

The exciting thing is we can accomplish all this by actually doing *less* marketing. Over the last few years, the list of all the marketing activities we are told to do has become never-ending. But when you look at all the most successful marketers, what's most surprising is their not-to-do list rather than their to-do list. Their marketing is lean, simple, and smart.

Brand Marketing and Direct Response Marketing

Brand marketing is marketing that's not measurable (at least not without a lot of mental gymnastics). It's the aspirational images and slogans on billboards, the splashy commercials, and the stadium naming rights. No one (including you) has any idea which ad made you buy that can of Coke or those Nike shoes.

For a long time, the formula for brand marketing success has been to use ads to interrupt whatever people are watching, listening to, or reading.

The hope of brand marketers is that with enough exposure to their message, you'll choose them when it comes time to make a purchasing decision. Reaching more people with more repetition is the name of the game.

The profits from these interruption-based sales are reinvested into more ads, and the process gets repeated over and over. Many huge brands were built this way, and many fortunes were made as a result.

Brand marketers care deeply about their brand's image and how it's perceived. They want to be surrounded by an environment that aligns with their brand. That's why they're quick to pull sponsorship or ad dollars from anything controversial.

Building a mass-market brand requires large investments and years to get results. Postwar Japan didn't have the resources to invest in mass manufacturing. Similarly, most small- and medium-sized businesses don't have the resources to do mass marketing. They need a smarter, leaner approach.

Direct response marketing is the other major class of marketing. It's action-based and almost scientific in its use of measurement. It's advertising that's designed to pay for itself. It's targeted and tracked.

Direct response marketers use highly measurable mediums like pay-per-click ads, direct mail, and email. They measure every action: the click, the opt-in, the purchase. Return on investment calculations are tangible and based on shorter time horizons.

They care a lot less about how they're perceived or where the ad is run. It's the metrics and the return on ad spend that matter most. They care about the 1 percent of people who saw their ad and clicked. They don't care about the other 99 percent and burn a lot of goodwill in the process.

Of course, nothing in life is completely black or white.

Brand marketers will tell you about metrics like "brand lift"— the likelihood of someone recognizing or interacting with a brand after seeing the ad. This is nice, but you have to squint hard to see a connection to the bottom line.

Measurement, though a source of pride in direct response marketing, can also be challenging. For example, if you clicked on a digital ad, opted in on a landing page, got three emails over the course of a week, and saw a retargeting ad, which one of these made you buy? The initial ad? The email nurturing? The retargeting ad? All of them combined? If it was all of them combined, do we assign them all equal weight? That's why some direct response marketers employ data scientists to create attribution models.

Brand marketing is subject to the John Wanamaker rule: "Half the money I spend on advertising is wasted; the trouble is I don't know which half." This is worlds away from the precision, discipline, and efficiency of lean thinking. Can you imagine someone in manufacturing ever saying, "Half the money we spend on raw materials is wasted; the trouble is we don't know which half"? That doesn't happen. Factories that operate at Six Sigma standards produce less than 3.4 defects per million opportunities. This is an incredible example that the world of marketing could learn from.

Does this mean brand marketing sucks and direct response marketing is the way to go? No. We'd be intellectually dishonest if we dismissed a strategy used by some of the world's biggest and most successful organizations. Great brands create powerful stories, build enormous goodwill, and occupy space in people's minds.

This becomes an incredibly efficient way to create customers and generate revenue, particularly at scale. It's instructive that while many companies start with direct response, they move more towards brand marketing as they scale. It's unusual to see huge companies primarily based on direct response marketing. It does happen, but it's rare.

By paying attention to the principles that have been perfected over decades in lean thinking and lean manufacturing, we can make branding efforts less wasteful and, therefore, use them at a smaller scale. We can also take the relentlessly profit-focused principles of direct response marketing, make them more brand-friendly, and use them at a larger scale.

The Best Marketing Book I Have Ever Read

I was recently the keynote speaker at an industry conference. Partway through my presentation, I held up a copy of my book *The 1-Page Marketing Plan* and said, "This is the best marketing book I have ever read—I wrote it." This got a few laughs, partly because of the shameless braggadocio and partly because they weren't quite sure if my quip was serious.

And while that may have been a little on the boastful side, you have no idea how many emails and messages I've received from readers saying those exact same words to me: "This is the best marketing book I have ever read."

It has to do with how that book came about. It's not a book I wrote for self-promotion or to make a lot of money (although it has done both of those things). *The 1-Page Marketing Plan* was the book I wished was available when I was learning marketing for the first time—when I was a dead-broke IT guy without any idea how to market myself. I wrote it for my past, clueless self and, in the process, helped a lot of people who were in the same position I was.

I've never been a fan of fake humility—the kind that mealy-mouthed politicians are famous for. When I do something I'm proud of, I call it out. That way, I have at least one fan of my work. I still stand by that statement but add to it this book, as it continues where *The 1-Page Marketing Plan* left off.

If your goal is to win the war, your strategy is all about how you'll get there in broad terms. For example, "We're going to drive the enemy back to its borders." Your tactics will be what you will do in specific terms, like, "We're going to bomb their tanks and cut off their supply lines."

Strategy is about priorities and allocating your finite resources for maximum impact. Tactics are all about execution and the specific actions, techniques, and maneuvers you'll use to carry out the strategy effectively.

The 1-Page Marketing Plan was highly focused on strategy. We did touch on some tactical stuff, but it was primarily concerned with strategy because that's what you need first.

This book is much more tactical, while still being self-contained. You'll get enormous value from reading it on its own. Paired with *The 1-Page Marketing Plan*, I'm certain you'll feel like it's 1 + 1 = 3. Together, they're like a street-smart MBA in marketing.

Putting Your Plan Into Action

This book is divided into four main parts. I start with Foundations (this part), where we'll cover some basics such as target market and product-market fit. Without these, the tactics won't work well. Even if a lot of it is familiar to you, a refresher can be helpful. If you already have a solid grasp of these or are impatient to get to the tactical portion of the book, then feel free to skip ahead to Chapter 4.

Product-market fit is about meeting real customer needs in a way that is (or is perceived to be) better than the alternatives. It's the right stuff for the right people. Marketing is an amplifier, so if your foundations are questionable, your results will be even more so when they're amplified. A bad singer with a good microphone is just a loud, bad singer, which makes things worse.

So Chapters 2 and 3 are about getting your product-market fit right so that you're amplifying something that your audience wants to hear.

However, don't make the common mistake of turning this into a point of procrastination and paralysis by analysis. Too many smart people think they're measuring twice and cutting once, but often they never cut. They just measure forever.

Accept that your product-market fit may be imperfect at first. You'll need to course-correct or even pivot along the way as you get more and better information.

Applying the Three Force Multipliers

Once, I was running a workshop and started by asking the audience, "Who wants to double their business profit?" Cheap audience engagement trick, I know.

A large number of enthusiastic hands shot up. "It's easy," I said, "just double the number of hours you work." I saw deflated faces and hands dropping back down.

Even if you do manage to double the number of hours you work, you can only perform that trick once, maybe twice, if you currently work very little. Then, your health, relationships, and other things start to suffer. Plus, there's the minor matter of there being only 24 hours in a day.

The only way to multiply your business results without multiplying the time and resources you put in is with leverage—a recurring theme of this book. Linear thinking gives you incremental gains. Leveraged thinking gets you *exponential* results.

So, what is leverage, exactly? Leverage is anything that multiplies the force of your inputs. If you can put one unit of time, money, or energy in and get more than one unit back out, that's leverage at work. Leverage is a force multiplier.

The tactical portion of this book covers the three force multipliers you'll need to build a powerful marketing infrastructure: Tools, Assets, and Processes. Each of these force multipliers is covered in its own part.

Tools are our first force multiplier. Tools are what sets our species apart from all others. The invention and use of business tools has been responsible for huge gains in productivity and wealth. Similarly, the right marketing tools help you punch above your weight. They're also critical in helping you create, deploy, and manage your marketing assets and processes. The Tools part of this book isn't a comprehensive deep dive into every marketing tool you'll need because that would be mind-numbingly boring. Also, discussing tools in isolation often doesn't make much sense. Instead, I'll talk about the various tools you'll need as and when they're relevant throughout.

Assets are our second force multiplier. Assets are how the wealthy generate income and get wealthier. It's also how great marketers generate a constant flow of leads, prospects, and customers. For your marketing results to outpace your time, effort, and budget, you'll need to build marketing assets.

Processes are our third force multiplier. They're like algorithms you run in your business. Creating and deploying daily, weekly, and monthly marketing processes will help you get outsized results. Just as the magic of compound interest helps financial investments grow, the compounding gains of your marketing processes will fuel your business growth.

Together, tools, assets, and processes help you create a devastatingly effective marketing system—one that allows you to get bigger results with fewer inputs.

There's so much pressure to do more marketing—more complex, more aggressive, and more expensive marketing. I think you'll find the contrarian simplicity of lean marketing refreshing.

Nothing New

My work has sometimes been criticized as "nothing new" or just "common sense." Largely I agree—but having seen inside thousands of businesses, I can also tell you that common sense is not common practice.

For example, capturing the email addresses of visitors to your website (discussed in Chapter 9) is nothing new. It's a simple, common-sense idea, but the vast majority of businesses don't do it. Content marketing (discussed in Chapter 13) is another idea that's not new, but again, few businesses do it consistently or well.

There's clearly a large gap between knowledge and implementation, one I hope this book will help you close. We'll take simple, common-sense ideas and dive into the details needed to actually implement them.

Through expensive experience, I've learned that simple scales and fancy fails.

Want to lose weight? Consume fewer calories than you expend.

Want to get strong? There's nothing new here either: most of your results will come from a few basic movements like the squat, deadlift, and bench press. You might say that's not original, and you'd be right, but it's effective. If you want to be original, stand on your head if you like. But that's not going to get you strong.

I won't be offended if you think of me like a fitness trainer—effective but not necessarily original. I don't care about being original. I just want you to get results.

I'll let the real fitness trainers train your body. I'm here to train your marketing muscle, and most of your results will come from only a handful of "movements."

Whether you want to get bod or get bank, a solid grasp of the fundamentals is key to your success.

The Fundamental and the Technical

Books are a wonderful way to package fundamentals. They have a longevity that no other format has. We still read and treasure books from hundreds or even thousands of years ago.

Online articles, social media posts, or YouTube videos don't have the same durability. You read or watch them, in amongst all your other digital distractions, then 30 seconds later, you've forgotten them. A book gives you the time and space to think, focus, and learn.

But books have a serious downside. They're surprisingly difficult to update. There are many intermediaries involved, such as editors, typesetters, publishers, distributors, and retailers. Even minor corrections or updates to a book can become a project, and the entire process can take a long time. Because of this, it wouldn't make sense to include screenshots, templates, and technical how-to's inside this book. They'd be obsolete by the time you read them.

So, to get the best of both worlds, I'll cover the timeless fundamentals in this book, but I'll also point you to relevant external resources that will cover the ever-changing technical aspects of marketing. These external resources are housed in the Lean Marketing Hub and will be updated regularly by my team and me. Along the way, I'll include signposts leading you to these resources.

Go to LeanMarketing.com/hub to get free access to the Lean Marketing Hub. There you can access all the resources that go along with this book, ask questions, and take your journey into lean marketing further.

A lot of what's covered in this book answers the question that Jeff Bezos constantly asks: "What's going to stay the same?" The good news is *a lot*. As you'll see, improvements in technology have simplified and democratized the technical aspects of marketing. They're not the competitive advantage they once were. Your biggest wins in the marketplace will come from fundamentals.

Enough foreplay. Let's get started.

Chapter 1 Action Items

- Review all of your marketing activities. Note all the activities that don't create value for your target market.

- Review your entire customer journey. Make a note of opportunities to embed marketing throughout.

- Revisit your marketing plan. Use the 1-Page Marketing Plan canvas if you need a fast and easy way to do this (accessible for free inside the Lean Marketing Hub).

2

Who Are Your People?

CHAPTER 2 SUMMARY

Many entrepreneurs start by trying to find a market for their product or service. A key to your marketing success is first having a clear picture of your target market and a deep understanding of them.

Highlights covered in this chapter include:

- Why product-first thinking is sabotaging your marketing success

- How to use "talent stacking" to create a unique value proposition even if you're not unique or "the best" at what you do

- Why trying to generate demand is a battle you'll likely lose and what to do instead

- How to become irresistible to your target market through specificity

- A framework for tightly defining your target market through seven dimensions

- How to deeply understand your target market by going undercover

- How your past struggles and experiences are powerful tools for target market selection

Stuff for Your People, Not People for Your Stuff

I've been interviewed on many podcasts, and a typical question I get asked is, "What's the biggest marketing mistake people make?" My answer is almost always the same. People start with their product or service and then look for a market to sell into.

Your target market is a foundational element of your marketing strategy. I'm shocked by how many people have figured out what their product is but have no idea how to get customers. That's where companies go to die.

In Silicon Valley, they call this a solution in search of a problem. It's ass-backward, and it's going to cause you a lot of pain. You can't create a compelling message when you're unclear about the intended audience. A message that lands with one audience may fall flat with another.

You'll also waste a lot of money on ads that don't work if you're reaching the wrong audience, and sales conversion will be an uphill battle.

If you're experiencing any of these symptoms, it could be because you don't have a crystal-clear idea of your target market.

Good marketing is **stuff for your people, not people for your stuff**. Product comes after market. So, it's essential to figure out who your people are.

Think of yourself as the mayor of your town. What do your citizens need? Chances are the answer will differ significantly from town to town.

For example, certain things instantly come to mind when I think about where I live. There's a dangerous intersection that needs traffic lights installed. There are serious accidents there every year, and every morning, traffic gets backed up trying to turn onto the main road.

LEAN MARKETING PRINCIPLE 3:
Market comes before product

There's also a big problem with day-trippers who park illegally on the esplanade to access the beach and cliffs nearby. They're noisy, leave a lot of trash behind, and make things unpleasant for locals.

There are also things that the city council does well, like maintaining the forest areas and clearing away overgrown grass and dead trees to prevent wildfires. These things would be completely irrelevant in other towns. A good mayor makes decisions based on a knowledge of the needs of the local townspeople.

You're going to treat your target market the same way. You'll first get a crystal-clear picture of who they are and what problems they're experiencing. In this chapter, I'll give you some powerful tools to help you work this out.

An Inch Wide and a Mile Deep

I recently went away with some friends, and we tried clay shooting for the first time. Our instructor was a champion Olympic shooter. His most useful tip was to ignore the natural instinct of trying to follow the clay target as it gets launched. Instead, he instructed us to position our rifles to where the clay was headed, move the rifle as little as possible, and then shoot when the clay target appeared in the line of sight.

Similarly, most rookie entrepreneurs try to follow many target markets and end up missing them all. Maybe you're an accountant, lawyer, butcher, baker, candlestick maker, or whatever. Almost everyone can use your product or service, so it feels natural to cast the widest possible net to try to catch them all.

Selecting a very specific target market feels counterintuitive. Every instinct you have will be to try to expand your market and your product or service offering. But it's a mistake. Just like following a clay target inevitably results in a miss, so too will your efforts if you try to chase everyone and be all things to all people.

The path to domination starts with a narrow focus. Facebook was only in colleges for its first two years. Apple's comeback had only the iPod for six years.

Amazon may be "the everything store" today, but it started as an online bookstore. After three or four years, they dominated that category, then added music and videos, then toys, then electronics, then tools. You know the rest of the story. Had they started as "the everything store," they likely wouldn't exist today.

I'll often ask someone who thinks they've niched down what their target market is, and they'll say something like "women over 40 years old." Great, so that's narrowed it down to 1.5 billion people. What do we do with that?

While I wouldn't say you can't be too niche, chances are that when you think you've niched enough, you probably haven't.

You want your niche to be an inch wide and a mile deep. An inch wide means you target a very tightly defined segment or subsegment of a market. A mile deep means a large enough addressable market is looking for a solution to a specific problem.

This doesn't have to be a huge market. It just needs to be the right market for you. You can be successful beyond your wildest dreams, even if 99.9 percent of the planet has never heard of you.

The Woman in the Red Dress

I recently heard Alex Hormozi describe the distractions of chasing new markets and opportunities as "the woman in the red dress," a reference to the movie *The Matrix*. In one scene, Morpheus takes his trainee, Neo, through a virtual reality training program. They're walking through a crowded street full of people wearing drab, monochrome clothing, as Morpheus explains The Matrix to Neo. Then, a gorgeous woman in a bright red dress emerges from the oncoming crowd. She flashes Neo a sexy smile as she walks past, and he can't keep his eyes off her. Morpheus stops to bring Neo back from his distraction and asks if he's listening or looking at the woman in the red dress. He then tells him to turn around and look again. When he does, Agent Smith, a simulated bad guy, is pointing a gun at Neo's head—a reminder that distractions can be deadly.

If you run even a mildly successful business, you'll constantly have distractions, new opportunities, and bright, shiny objects coming at you. Every fiber of your being will beg you to widen the net, expand your offering, and follow the sexy and new. They're the woman in the red dress. As you become more and more successful, she keeps coming back and seems more and more attractive each time because you're presented with increasingly bigger and better opportunities.

As entrepreneurs, novelty is in our DNA. The new idea, new product, new market. I'm by no means immune to the seduction of the woman in the red dress either. I'm constantly reminding myself to stay focused on our current opportunities because focus and energy are finite resources.

Imagine you have ten units of energy. If you scatter it in ten different directions, you'll make one unit of progress in each. But if you focus all ten units of energy in a single direction, you'll get ten units of progress in that direction.

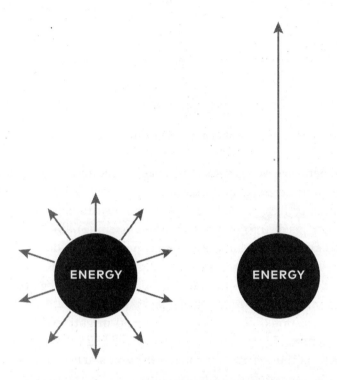

In the marketplace, you're competing against people who have put all their units of energy in a single direction. While there are some very rare people who are so talented they can execute multiple things at once at a high level, you should assume you're not one of them. Assume, like most who've succeeded, that you'll need to make trade-offs. A lot of them.

Two things have helped me deal with the woman in the red dress and maintain my focus. First, a "parking lot" for future ideas, business ventures, and products. That way, I don't feel like they're lost—they're still there for a future time when I have the capacity to deal with them. In reality, I couldn't execute all the products, ideas, and ventures I have in my parking lot in ten lifetimes. But it still feels better than just discarding them.

The second thing that's been helpful is seeing so many businesses from the inside. From the outside, a lot of markets and businesses look very profitable and easy. When I see what's really involved and what actually falls to the bottom line, I'm rarely as enthusiastic. Many high-ticket, high-revenue businesses have low leverage and sucky business models.

Specificity Sells, Generality Repels

Specificity sells, and generality repels. I can prove this to you in five seconds. Go to your smartphone or computer and look at your search history. Now, focus on the search terms related to something you considered purchasing. Marketers often refer to these keywords as having "commercial intent." Notice that your searches are very specific.

You probably didn't type "doctor" or "car" into the search box. You're much more likely to have typed something like "dermatologist downtown Brooklyn" or "which Porsche 911 models have all-wheel drive?"

Knowing the specific search terms your market uses is critical to the success of your inbound marketing. You'll never get to such specifics if your targeting is too broad.

Being specific and targeted is a great way of optimizing your product or service for maximum profit. You'll see this in the personal care industry. Products like deodorants or razors have versions for men and women. The actual products are often identical, except the men's are packaged in blue or black, and those targeted at women are pink. This causes most households to buy both. Further, the ones targeted at women often attract a so-called pink tax because they're priced higher than the men's versions. I simultaneously despise and admire this tactic. I despise it because I'm against gender discrimination. I admire it because it's additional margin that falls directly to the bottom line, a truly beautiful thing that warms my heart. High margins are my love language.

A similar thing is done with the pain relief medication sold in most drug stores. You'll find a box of general pain relief medication on the shelf, alongside variants "targeted" at specific pains such as headaches, period cramps, backaches, sinus issues, and arthritis. Except, there's no such thing as selectively targeting pain in specific body parts. The active ingredient, such as acetaminophen or ibuprofen, is identical across these products. The main differences are in the packaging and price.

Why would they go to so much trouble to pay for different printing, packaging, and shelf space? Because they know if you've got back pain, the package that says "Relief for Back Pain" will make you say, "That's for me," grab it off the shelf, and head to the checkout.

You want your products or services to have a similar effect on your market—targeting a specific pain point so they say, "That's for me."

Nothing Is So Unequal as the Equal Treatment of Unequal People

A common question I get asked is, "Do I need a separate marketing plan for each of my target markets?" The answer depends on whether you truly have different target markets or if they're just segments of an existing market.

Even if you only have a single target market, it's smart to segment it. As I expressed earlier, a message that really lands with one audience may fall flat with another.

Treating different audiences equally and nurturing them the same way is a huge marketing mistake and leads to a lot of waste— wasted time, money, and effort. Irrelevant marketing creates no value for your customer or prospect and undermines your brand instead of enhancing it.

For example, if you manufacture baby products, you may have multiple distribution channels. You may sell direct-to-consumer (D2C) from your online store but also have a wholesale channel where you sell to retailers, who onsell your products to consumers.

So, how do we determine if retailers and consumers are separate target markets with their own marketing plans or segments of the same market? Things I would consider include:

- Will they respond to vastly different messages?

- Will my advertising media differ significantly between them?

- Will my nurturing process be different?

- What will my sales process look like for each of these?

- How will I manage the short-term onboarding and long-term customer management processes for each one?

In this example, they would likely respond to significantly different messages. A baby's parent wants to know the product is safe and will do what it promises to do.

A retailer will also care about these things, but it's probably not going to be the message that really captures their attention. A retailer will get excited if you tell them about the high margin they'll make, how hot the product is with consumers, and the high sell-through rates they can expect. The messaging will be vastly different.

We'll also likely use different advertising media. To get in front of our consumer market, we might use pay-per-click ads and user-generated content on social media. To capture retailers, we'd likely advertise in trade publications or send sales reps to industry trade shows.

The nurturing process is also quite different. Consumers may need little or no nurturing, buying the product on impulse or because it meets an immediate need. By contrast, dealing with distributors and getting shelf space with retailers will likely make for a long sales cycle.

The sales process with consumers would just be encouraging them to add the item to their cart and then enter their credit card details on the checkout page. Meanwhile, the sales process with retailers would include a lengthy process of signing a supply agreement, negotiating credit terms, and integrating with their procurement and logistics systems.

Tap Into Demand

I chuckled the first few times I heard the job title "Demand Generation Manager." Most businesses can't generate demand any more than they can generate the sun rising.

Your aim is to *tap into* demand rather than trying to *generate* it. You want to be like a solar panel absorbing the sun's rays and turning them into usable energy as efficiently as possible.

It is possible to generate demand, but it's very difficult, very expensive, and takes a very long time. In 1873, Colgate launched the first-ever commercially manufactured toothpaste. For a long time after, toothbrushing was mostly something that only fancy rich people did. It wasn't the universal routine it is today. Colgate spent decades and millions of dollars convincing consumers that their breath stinks. The practice of toothbrushing finally became widespread after the Second World War. That's an example of truly generating demand.

When the student is ready, the teacher will arrive—in other words, you can't make someone accept a message they aren't ready to receive. A few short years ago, I had absolutely zero interest in health, nutrition, or fitness. When I saw a shirtless, muscular gym junkie walk past, I'd snicker to myself, "Meathead." You could have had the best fitness program or nutrition product on the planet, and I wouldn't have given it a second look. You could have given it to me for free, and I wouldn't have taken it. The student wasn't ready.

Now, health and wellness are things I care deeply about. The student is now ready. I spend a ton of money on good nutrition, personal trainers, and gym equipment. I subscribe to courses and get advice from biohackers. Articles on the topic get my attention, and ripped dudes get my admiration because I now know what it takes to get there.

If you've ever tried to change someone's behavior, even when it's good for them, you know what a challenge that is. If you're trying to do that in the marketplace, you're playing business in hard mode.

You may have awesome stuff, but if you're selling it to the wrong people, it'll fall flat. Too many people are trying to sell binoculars to the blind. When they get resistance, they feel like that's their cue to push harder and highlight features and benefits.

By going where people are already looking, you'll always have more success than you would by trying to make them look at you. Tap into existing, unsatisfied demand.

Even within a market where demand exists, it will have varying intensities. In his classic book *Breakthrough Advertising*, Eugene Schwartz talks about the five stages of customer awareness:

1 **Unaware:** Someone who doesn't even know they have a problem.

2 **Problem aware:** Someone who has a problem but doesn't know there are solutions to that problem.

3 **Solution aware:** Someone who knows there are solutions but hasn't chosen one and doesn't know about your solution or product.

4 **Product aware:** Someone who knows about your solution or product but isn't sure it solves their problem or hasn't selected you from your competitors.

5 **Most aware:** Someone who knows a lot about your solution or product. They're on the cusp of buying but need to know the specifics.

The **unaware** are usually not worth marketing to. Trying to convince them they have a problem will be an uphill battle. If you have something truly unique (which is risky) and insist on a life of frustration and pain, then the best way to connect with the unaware is by echoing an emotion or attitude they can identify with. Many inventor types live in this world and usually die poor and disillusioned.

Someone who's **problem aware** is in pain or knows they have a problem but doesn't yet know about any potential solutions (including yours). These are excellent targets for content marketing (discussed in Chapter 13). Their search queries often start with "how to," followed by their desired outcome.

Solution aware prospects are slightly warmer. They know they have a problem and know that solutions exist but are unaware of you. A typical search query for someone at this stage would be something like "best luxury SUV with 7 seats." These prospects are good candidates for content marketing that gives them a tool or resource to help them measure or understand their problem in a way that lines them up for your solution. Your flagship asset (discussed in Chapter 8) is excellent for this.

Product aware people would be considered warm leads. They're aware they have a problem, they know you have a potential solution to it, but they're unsure if what you have will solve their problem. They're likely comparing you to other competing solutions. A search term by someone who's product aware might be something like "BMW X7 vs Range Rover." Lead nurturing is essential for these prospects. Proof, testimonials, and demonstrating how good their life will be with your solution are also important.

The **most aware** are hot leads. They know what you do. They know you solve their problems, and they want your solution. They may just need an incentive, a reason, or a deal to buy. Typical search terms may be "Best deal for a BMW X7 in San Francisco." Strong calls to action, fear of missing out, and guarantees can be useful in getting them across the line.

Your Niche Is at the Intersection

Strong niches blend several broader elements. If you do something very general and want to get a lot of attention, you'll need to be exceptional at it. That's kind of a problem for most people because being exceptional means that almost nobody is at that level. You're literally an exception.

For example, Jamaican sprinter Usain Bolt won the 100-meter dash at the 2009 World Athletics Championships in Berlin with a time of 9.58 seconds.

Was the fourth-place runner—the guy who didn't even get a bronze medal—five seconds behind Usain? Two seconds? One second? Turns out, he was only a few tenths of a second behind him. But that 0.35 of a second meant the difference between standing on the podium, achieving world fame, earning millions of dollars in sponsorship and prize money, and leaving empty-handed and living a life of obscurity.

From this, there's both good news and bad news.

Being the best in the world at whatever you do is one way to stand out from the crowd, but it's incredibly hard to do and will take Olympic athlete–like dedication. And even then, there aren't any guarantees of success. That's the bad news.

The good news is that you don't have to be the world's best to get your customers a great result, create a lot of value in the marketplace, and live an incredible lifestyle. The guy who finished in fourth place is still an amazing runner.

If you're an accountant, you don't need to be the world's best to get your clients awesome results. But if you want to capture their attention and stand out from every other accountant, you'll need to do better than just tell them about saving money on their taxes, which is what every accountant does.

In *Get Different,* my friend Mike Michalowicz wrote, "Better is not better. Different is better." A great way to be completely differentiated is by talent stacking. This places you at the intersection of multiple different things. You then don't have to be the greatest at any one of those things.

This is done with food all the time—for example, jumbo donuts. You don't need to make the world's best donuts. You'll get immediate attention because they're huge. Other food examples are green ketchup or cookie dough ice cream.

This book and my work are examples of talent stacking and finding that intersection.

Am I the world's greatest writer? I assure you I am not.

Am I sidesplittingly hilarious? Put it this way. If Dave Chappelle and I are ever in town at the same time and you're in the difficult position of having to choose between seeing his comedy show and attending one of my keynotes, do yourself a favor and see the Dave Chappelle show.

Am I the greatest technology mind on the planet? I am not.

Am I the world's best at breaking down complex concepts and presenting them simply? I'm OK, but I'm at least one Nobel Prize short of the likes of Richard Feynman.

But if I stack them all together, I arrive at a reasonably unique intersection. I simplify the complex for entrepreneurs and business leaders, give them easy-to-follow frameworks and systems, arm them with powerful technology tools, and wrap it all in an easy-to-follow and (hopefully) entertaining package.

Dharmesh Shah, the billionaire founder of HubSpot, described it as the Venn diagram of success. It goes something like this:

Imagine a giant whiteboard with a dot representing each human on Earth. There'd be about 8 billion dots on this whiteboard.

We draw a circle around all the people who are good at writing. Let's be generous and say it's 10 percent. So 800 million people. That's a lot of competition.

Then, we draw another circle around all the people with strong business knowledge. Again, being generous, let's say it's 1 percent.

We draw a third circle around all the people who understand systems, technology, and software tools at a deep level. Let's say 5 percent.

Finally, we draw a circle around all the people willing to undergo the unreasonable difficulty and pain involved in writing and publishing a nonfiction book. At most, this would be 0.05 percent of the population.

The number of dots inside the intersection of these four circles would be incredibly small. My guess is that it may be a total of 100 dots. So, my worldwide "competition" is about 100 other authors in my space. I personally know about 30 of them, and we don't consider ourselves competitors because multiple people can win this game. In fact, we frequently share ideas and promote each other's books.

(It's awesome authors like Mike Michalowicz, David Jenyns, Todd Herman, John Jantsch, Dan Martell, and Daniel Priestley. You should buy all their books.)

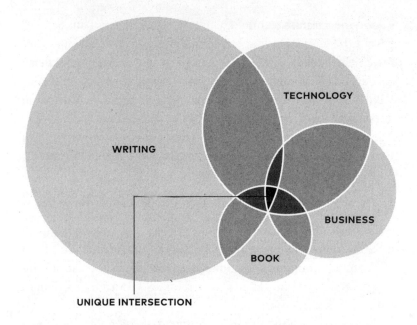

UNIQUE INTERSECTION

The other part of this is that we're not just stacking random skills. We're stacking skills that reinforce and enhance each other as much as possible.

If you stack highly unrelated skills, like scuba diving and knitting, you'll have trouble finding a point where they intersect. You may have little to no competition but also little to no demand. I'm not sure how much knitwear enhances the scuba diving experience, but I suspect not much.

If you're picking skills to learn, I recommend learning skills that are rare but also reinforce and enhance things that you're already reasonably good at. This is what creates enormous value.

The good news is that you're already doing this. Becoming better at marketing and influence is a skill that reinforces and enhances almost every aspect of your business and life.

By stacking skills, you don't have to be the best at either, just dangerous enough at each. In the land of the blind, the one-eyed man is king.

7 Ways to Niche

When narrowing down your target market, it can be helpful to look at it in a multidimensional way. Here are the seven dimensions I consider when helping someone choose their inch-wide but mile-deep niche.

1 **Location or geography:** for example, San Diego, the American Midwest, Australia, Vancouver

2 **Demography:** for example, baby boomers, British expats, 35–45-year-olds, divorcées, women

3 **Shared values:** for example, philanthropy, adrenaline junkies, faith, environmentalism, love of travel

4 **Industry:** for example, dental, legal, construction, IT managed services

5 **Desire:** for example, people who want to write a book, import products from China, apply for a government grant

6 **Problem:** for example, anxiety, accountability, low energy, financial stress

7 **Trend:** for example, medicinal psychedelics, secular spirituality, digital currencies, biohacking, artificial intelligence (AI)

You can use one of these dimensions, but often it's most powerful to use multiple. For example, you could be the accountant who serves British expats in Australia or the lawyer in California who advises software companies on AI-related legal issues.

There's a much higher likelihood that someone will say, "That's for me," if what you do is specific to their needs. You can imagine someone in these target markets is far more likely to do a specific search like "Do I need to declare my UK pension in Australia?" or "Does generative AI violate copyright law?" rather than "accountant" or "lawyer."

An important consideration is whether your niche or sub-niche is growing, shrinking, or stable. Tapping into a growing segment or subsegment gives you a nice tailwind.

Tapping into one that's growing in both size and affluence is like a cheat code. For example, couples with a double income and no kids (also known as DINKs) are a growing and affluent demographic. A variation is DINKWADs (double income, no kids, with a dog). Outside of the obvious spending on their fur babies, they also spend a lot on personal services, convenience, entertainment, and tech.

Demographic trends and shifts like these are worth paying attention to and can be a significant factor in your success.

Serve the Person You Once Were

My dad's sudden death kicked off my midlife crisis. I spent three long years in the abyss. During this time, I re-examined every part of my life: declining health, low energy, fracturing marriage, mediocre work output, and shattered faith. I was both physically and mentally weak.

I'll spare you the details, but I clawed my way out. I cleaned up my diet, strengthened my body and mind, fixed my marriage, and got focused on the most impactful projects in my business. Using books, courses, coaches, and consultants, I learned a lot of stuff about a lot of stuff and solved many of my problems in the process.

I'm certainly no expert in the fields where I overcame many of my midlife challenges, but with all that I've learned and been through, I'm confident I could guide someone with similar challenges to a better place.

In fact, my past deficiency in marketing is how I came to be doing what I do today. My struggle to get clients in my first business led me on a long and expensive journey to figuring out marketing. Now, I use that hard-won experience to help others shortcut that process.

When you've been in your prospect's shoes, it's a lot easier to have empathy. You can much more easily tap into their emotions and thoughts because you've been there. Your messaging becomes much more powerful as you enter the conversation taking place in their minds. It's also very satisfying and motivational, which is a nice side benefit.

I once heard Rory Vaden put it much more eloquently. He said, "You are most powerfully positioned to serve the person you once were." I love that. When choosing a target market or segment, you'll have a big advantage if you've had firsthand experience with their struggles.

Go Undercover

Sometimes you see an opportunity—an underserved market or segment of a market—but don't have the advantage of having been one of them. That's a challenge but not insurmountable. Here's how I recommend you think about it.

Imagine you're a spy whose top-secret mission is to infiltrate a target market and gather as much intelligence as possible. What would you do? Search engines are a good starting point, but real market research must go beyond a few basic search queries.

Come on—you're the country's top spy, and the president has personally tasked you with infiltrating this target market and producing deep, actionable insights. What are their dreams? What are their desires? What are they afraid of? What's motivating them? What are their strengths and weaknesses? What are their biases? Your country is depending on you and the quality of your intelligence gathering. Here's what I would do.

First, I'd start by finding out where they congregate online to chat. Certain target markets and subcultures tend to gravitate to certain platforms. The most common are Facebook Groups, X (formerly Twitter), Reddit, LinkedIn, and Discord. Don't discount older-style online forums and message boards either. Despite their aging looks and dated feel, many very active communities still live on these. For example, Hacker News is a message board where a lot of software startups exchange news, share ideas, and endlessly debate all sorts of minutiae. Gamers are very active on Discord.

I'm obsessed with Reddit. You can go deep into almost any sub-culture there. Posting a question often gets voluminous responses. Because it's mostly anonymous or pseudonymous, people tend to be much more open and honest there. There are "subreddits" on practically anything you can think of and many things you don't want to think about. There are subreddits dedicated to discussing everything from investment strategies to the most intimate details of people's sex lives. Many subreddits are dedicated to the trivial and nonsensical, while others go deep into the dark crevices of human behavior and psychology.

Private Facebook Groups are another valuable place to do online research. Because people there mostly use their real names and profile photos, you tend to get more shallow discussions, but it varies from group to group. While Reddit skews slightly towards the nerdy, Facebook Groups tend to skew towards lower-tech communities. There are very active groups about products, people, local communities, and almost anything else you can think of. Many businesses and products use Facebook Groups as a community add-on, so it can be a great place to get insights into the pain points of your competitor's customers.

Next, I'd look at podcasts, books, and YouTube channels. Most niches or sub-niches tend to have a few dominant thought leaders. They've often written the "classic" book for that industry or niche, and sometimes they also produce content and do interviews on podcasts and YouTube. These are valuable, but be aware that there's a performance element when people are being interviewed in formats for public consumption. They'll usually give an airbrushed version of the situation.

Next, I would look into industry trade journals or newsletters. Some of these are still in print, while most have moved online. Many of these are paywalled or require a subscription, but if you plan on getting into a market, it's well worth subscribing to get a deeper understanding of it. These publications are often very specific and are found in practically every niche, from waste management to teaching doctors how to invest their money.

I like these because you get very topical information that people in the industry find valuable enough to pay for. Also, you get to see who the advertisers and sponsors are in that industry and what pain points their offers are targeted to. Long-standing advertisers and sponsors are worth paying attention to because they're likely getting a good return on their ad spend. And if there isn't a trade journal or newsletter in the niche you're looking at, then start one!

Finally, I'll leave you with my best "hack" for getting up to speed on a target market in a very short period of time. Go to in-person conferences, trade shows, or industry association events. I've done this many times, and within a day, I know more about an industry, its pain points, and what the hot topics are than if I had spent six months doing online research.

The keynote speakers will usually be the who's who of the industry. The speeches, presentations, and panel discussions will center on the industry's hot-button issues. Chatting with other attendees will give you insights that would be very difficult to obtain as an outsider. Like Facebook Groups and Reddit subreddits, there are conferences on almost every conceivable topic, niche, and industry. This is a super-powerful way to accelerate your market research.

Whether you're doing online or offline research, your goal is to understand your target market at a deep level. Knowing their hopes, dreams, desires, and fears and tapping into their most pressing pain points will massively improve the effectiveness of your marketing efforts.

Pearls Before Swine

I'm fascinated with the simple idea that by serving a better market, you can charge orders of magnitude more for the exact same product or service because they value what you do much more.

I frequently see skilled entrepreneurs casting their pearls before swine. They have an incredible skill or solution but are selling it to a market that doesn't value what they do. Huge breakthroughs often come from pivots in their target market or segment.

This directly affects how easy it is to make the sale and how much someone is willing to pay you for what you do. Solving a problem is important, but applying it to the right market is where the money is made.

I recently saw a guy who was very skilled at generating social media buzz with powerful story-based content. But his real genius was finding a market that would value his work the most and pay accordingly. For him, it was companies about to be listed on the stock exchange. A good story can swing their valuation by hundreds of millions or even billions of dollars. He would take a small equity position in the company in exchange for his work. This often resulted in a multimillion-dollar payday after they were listed.

Many people with the same skills as him make a tiny fraction of what he makes because they're trying to get blood out of a stone. They're selling their services to the local coffee shop or dry cleaner, who may not value their work or have the capacity to pay. Strategically selecting your target market can mean doing the same work but with many more zeros.

A good angler doesn't just know how to fish. He knows where the best fishing spots are. Selecting the right target market is the first foundational factor in your marketing success. What you sell that target market will be the second. Let's look at that next.

Chapter 2 Action Items

- Stack your skills, experiences, and knowledge in a way that makes you unique and valuable to a specific target market.

- Consider if your target market is too broad. Use multiple niche dimensions to tightly define your target market.

- Go undercover and gather intelligence and insights into your target market both online and in person.

3

What Are You (Really) Selling?

CHAPTER 3 SUMMARY

Many marketers expend enormous resources on communicating the features and benefits of their products or services. Understanding the psychology of human desires and how it drives buying behavior is a much more powerful approach.

Highlights covered in this chapter include:

- Getting to the heart of what's motivating your target market using the Five Whys technique

- The seven core commodities that drive all buying behavior

- The four levers that will create value that your market will pay for even if what you sell is a commodity

- How deliberate positioning can differentiate you in a crowded marketplace

- The key role that your pricing plays in making your product or service attractive to your target market

- How to set your prices on the utility-signaling spectrum

- How "the velvet rope" turns customers into fans and evangelists of your product or service

The Holy Grail

You're just about to launch a new restaurant. A combination of excitement and nervousness is coursing through your body. As luck would have it, you stumble upon a magic lamp. You rub it, and a genie pops out and says, "Hey entrepreneur, I'm here to grant you one wish, any wish you like." What do you ask for? A great location? A Michelin star chef? An amazing new food concept? These are all nice-to-haves, but what you really want is a starving crowd.

Product-market fit is a term coined by renowned entrepreneur and venture capitalist Marc Andreessen. He writes, "In a great market—a market with lots of real potential customers—the market pulls product out of the startup."

The concept of customer *pull* is a key component of lean thinking. The customer pulls, or demands, products, services, or solutions to their problems from you rather than you pushing them, often unwanted, onto the customer.

Most entrepreneurs have a love affair with their product or service and an obsession with their competitors. Being overly concerned about competitors creates unnecessary anxiety and dilutes your focus. Most businesses that fail die of starvation, not murder.

Some entrepreneurs claim their product or service is so unique that no competitors exist. This is rarely true, and when it is, it's a huge red flag indicating low demand.

Product-market fit isn't defined by you or your competitors. Your customers define it. This is much more important than having "the best" product or service because it creates a demand-side pulling force.

I think it would be fair to say Starbucks doesn't have the best coffee, McDonald's doesn't have the best burgers, and Apple doesn't have the best consumer electronics. But each has built a massively successful business on the back of strong product-market fit and demand-side pull. Now it's time for you to do the same.

Your awesome product or service is a customer *retention* tool, which is important, but good marketing is a customer *acquisition* tool, and you need that first. No one knows how good your product or service is until after the sale. Before they buy, they only know how good your *marketing* is. Put simply, **the best marketer wins every time**. A foundational element to winning the game of marketing is product-market fit.

When you lack product-market fit, it feels like rolling a boulder uphill. Marketing can help, but it will be difficult, and you'll have to push hard to get each sale over the line.

When you have strong product-market fit, the boulder is rolling downhill. You're harnessing the natural inertia of demand. Here, marketing acts as an accelerator and helps you gain massive velocity. This is the holy grail.

Moist Robots

Many highly intelligent people are convinced that we're living inside a simulation—like characters in a video game or a virtual reality environment. It's a thought that crosses my mind often.

Maybe it's the nerd in me, but I see algorithms everywhere. A dog scratching itself, a person sneezing, the sun rising. These all seem like algorithms that run in response to an input or time-based trigger, just like computers do.

I'm also fascinated by how predictable human behavior is. That's the premise of the field of psychology, I suppose—to describe, predict, and modify that behavior. If we were all completely different and unpredictable, this wouldn't be a field of study.

It's like we're walking, talking computers. We have "hardware," our bodies. We also have "software," our minds. To borrow a term from Scott Adams, we're "moist robots."

Our hardware and software can let us down, support us, and, to some extent, be upgraded. Think of this book as an important "software update."

When you want a computer or robot to do something, you give it instructions through computer code. When you want a human being to do something, you use words. With the right combination of words, I believe you can "program" anyone to do almost anything.

In Chapter 5, I'll cover in much more detail how to use the right combination of words to program moist robots.

For now, let's look at the seven core commodities that drive all human behavior.

The Only Things Humans Buy or Sell

When I ask entrepreneurs what they sell, they usually describe their product or service and how it works. That's a nice start and explains the means to the end, but what I'm much more interested in is the end. What are you *really* selling?

The Five Whys is a problem-solving technique developed as a key component of the Toyota Production System and is commonly used in lean thinking and lean manufacturing. The technique involves asking "why" five times to uncover the root cause of a problem rather than focusing on the symptoms or immediate issues. By digging deeper into the problem, the Five Whys method helps to identify the root cause and develop more effective, long-lasting solutions.

Here's an example of the Five Whys technique applied to a production line in a factory that's frequently experiencing downtime.

Why is the production line experiencing downtime? Because a critical machine is malfunctioning.

Why is the machine malfunctioning? Because it's overheating.

Why is it overheating? Because the cooling system is not working properly.

Why isn't the cooling system working properly? Because it's clogged with debris.

Why is the cooling system clogged with debris? Because there's no regular maintenance schedule for it.

So, the root cause of the downtime is a lack of a regular maintenance schedule for the cooling system.

The Five Whys technique is useful beyond manufacturing and technical troubleshooting. It's good at getting to the root of most human behavior. For example:

Why do you need financing? Because I'm buying a Mercedes-Benz S-Class.

Why are you buying a Mercedes-Benz S-Class? Because I've been wanting one for a long time.

Why have you been wanting one for a long time? Because driving one demonstrates success and wealth.

Why do you want to demonstrate your success and wealth? Because showcasing it will earn me respect and admiration from others.

Why do you want respect and admiration from others? Because it will raise my status amongst my peers.

I don't think there's anything magical about the Five Whys, but using an iterative interrogative technique gets you closer to the real essence of a thing.

When I ask, "What are you *really* selling?" it can take a few iterations of interrogation, but we'll eventually get to one or more of the following seven things:

1 Money and wealth

2 Time and convenience

3 Sex and mating

4 Status, fame, and approval

5 Safety, peace of mind, and basic needs

6 Leisure, entertainment, and play

7 Freedom

These seven core commodities are the *only* things people really buy or sell. They drive all human behavior.

To determine what drives buying behavior, ignore what people say they want but pay close attention to what they actually *do*. Truth in marketing is determined not by how people use their mouths but by how they use their wallets. That's why I'm not a big fan of focus groups or surveys. They can serve as a data point, but they're usually inaccurate because people lie to you and to themselves.

© marketoonist.com

Whenever you find yourself asking, "Why are they doing that?" or "Why am I doing this?" the answer is the pursuit of one or more of these core commodities. And whenever you find yourself asking, "How do I get this person to do what I want them to do?" the answer is the same.

Let's look at the core commodities in a bit more detail.

The 7 Core Commodities

Money and Wealth

Does it help them make or save money? Does it help protect or increase wealth?

The pursuit of wealth drives our economic engine and influences almost every decision we make.

While wealth and money are related, they're not the same thing. You can have wealth without having money.

Wealth is the stuff you want: food, clothes, houses, cars, travel to cool places, etc.

If you had a magic wand that you could wave and it would give you a car or cook you dinner or clean your house, or do anything else you wanted, you'd be the wealthiest person in the world, and you wouldn't need money.

Conversely, if you were stranded on a desert island with all the money in the world, it would be useless to you unless you could exchange it for the stuff you wanted.

In practice, money and wealth are often interchangeable, but what you, your prospects, and I really want is wealth.

Time and Convenience

Does it save time or energy?

While money is a renewable resource, time can't be regained once spent. It's our most valuable resource.

This makes time-saving convenience an immensely compelling driver of human behavior.

As Evan Williams, the co-founder of Twitter (now X), put it, "Convenience decides everything." Convenience very often makes our decisions for us, sometimes even overriding our innate preferences.

I prefer to walk or cycle, but driving my car is so convenient that it's my default form of transport. If I'm going to walk or cycle somewhere, I must consciously decide to do so.

I prefer to support independent retailers, but Amazon is so convenient that it's my default online shopping destination. Buying a product with one click and having it arrive today or tomorrow is compelling.

Convenience often makes other options seem ridiculous. Once you've used a washing machine, hand-washing your clothes seems irrational. After you've binge-watched a TV series on Netflix, waiting for a particular day and time to see the next episode of your show seems unthinkable. Resisting convenient time- and energy-saving devices even seems rather eccentric, like people who refuse to use email or own a cell phone.

You can get more of most things, but you can never get more time, which makes it an incredibly powerful driver of human behavior.

Sex and Mating

Does it help them find or make love?

The innate desire to reproduce governs the behavior of every living thing.

This is why the phrase "sex sells" is so deeply ingrained in modern advertising and media. Sex sells everything from CRM software to coffee. A quote often attributed to Oscar Wilde is, "Everything in the world is about sex, except sex. Sex is about power."

The notion of sex selling is not just a marketing gimmick but a reflection of deeply rooted biological and psychological factors.

FYI, reading this book makes you 37% sexier. ☺

Status, Fame, and Approval

Does it improve their status or help them gain approval?

Humans are social animals. Social hierarchy in humans (as in all primates) is hardwired. Being excluded from your tribe is possibly the harshest punishment you can receive. At one time, it could have even meant death.

People will go to incredible lengths for status, fame, or approval.

It should also be noted that status is highly contextual. You might have high status in one arena but be a nobody in another. For example, you might be the respected alpha dog in the boardroom, but step into a boxing ring and it's lights out in ten seconds.

An essential part of status is signaling it. I'll talk more about this shortly.

Safety, Peace of Mind, and Basic Needs

Does it provide peace of mind or reduce risk?

This encompasses physical and psychological safety, sufficient calories, hydration, shelter, warmth, and so on.

These basic needs are foundational. Our brains are wired for survival above all else and will pursue it relentlessly.

Leisure, Entertainment, and Play

Does it help them relax, recover, or escape?

Leisure, entertainment, and play are essential for human well-being. They have a crucial role in a balanced and fulfilling life. Far from being optional or superfluous, they contribute to cognitive, social, emotional, and physical development.

Leisure, entertainment, and play also facilitate social cohesion, connect us with others, and allow us to share experiences and pass down values, beliefs, and traditions across generations. They foster a sense of belonging and connection to the tribe.

Freedom

Does it enhance their sense of personal freedom?

If you had everything but your freedom to choose was taken away, you'd still be unhappy.

I think of those like royalty or heirs to family fortunes who have their life course predetermined. Despite immense wealth, power, status, and having all their needs taken care of, some still relinquish their duties due to a lack of freedom to pursue their own path.

Freedom and independence are the basis upon which many nations are founded. They're also an extremely common motivation of entrepreneurs.

Having an option forced upon you, even if it's a good one, severely detracts from its desirability. By contrast, when people have optionality, they feel much more positive about their decisions, even when they're suboptimal.

NOTE: Not all human desires can be packaged neatly. Many things have multidimensional drivers. For example, a car might fall under time and convenience, but it also has status, leisure, and freedom attached to it.

Like most commodities, the seven core commodities can also be traded for each other. Time is often traded for safety, freedom can be traded for status, and almost anything can be traded for money.

Vitamins and Painkillers

All personal development can be summarized as follows: prioritize the long term over the short term. So why don't we do this naturally? Why doesn't everyone exercise, save and invest for the future, eat well, and build meaningful relationships? It's because our brains are wired for survival, not success. Your brain doesn't care if you're successful or happy. It only cares if you survive. So when you're looking at a pizza loaded with calories, your brain thinks, "Awesome, lots of calories; we get to survive for a bit longer," and it signals you to eat.

For most people and for most of human history, survival was the major challenge, so this made sense. Eat, drink, and be merry, for tomorrow we may die. No longer facing a constant threat of death is a relatively recent phenomenon. Despite this, our brain is still hardwired for survival, safety, and pain avoidance. Benefits and thinking about the future are optional extras.

This is important information for marketers. If what you do is perceived by your target market as a vitamin—that is, something optional that may provide some future benefit—you'll have a much harder time selling it. You want them to perceive it as a painkiller, something that can be taken to relieve pain immediately.

Some people take this to mean that "painkillers" are essentials like food, water, and shelter, and so-called discretionary purchases are vitamins. This isn't true. Whether something is a vitamin or a painkiller is not determined by your product but by your market. For example, a Mercedes-Benz S-Class may be perceived as a vitamin by one market segment but as a painkiller by another.

Part of your work in finding product-market fit is finding the market that perceives what you do as a painkiller rather than a vitamin. It's the starving crowd when you have a restaurant. It's the person with a migraine when you sell pain relief medication.

Pain moves your market to action more effectively than pleasure. When you have a target market in desperate need of one or more of the seven core commodities in a form that you can satisfy with your product or service, it's magic. You have the all-important *product-market fit*.

Whatever your product or service is, it's just a delivery mechanism for one or more of the seven core commodities. Think of it as the gelatin capsule that holds the active ingredients in a pill. Someone who needs to raise or maintain their status within their peer group may buy a painkiller in the form of a Mercedes-Benz.

Which of the seven core commodities does your target market lack that your product or service can satisfy? That's a key question.

Most entrepreneurs spend their time shouting features and benefits at an indifferent audience. That's like trying to sell pain relief medication to someone who's never experienced a headache. Even worse, it's trying to sell them the delivery mechanism itself—the gelatin capsule—which they care about even less. Telling them all about the capsule, the color, and what it's made of will fall on deaf ears.

You'll rarely achieve product-market fit on your first try. It will usually take some iterations or pivots. I'll give you an example of this from my own business. A few years ago, in one of our coaching programs, we recognized that the business owner was almost always the bottleneck. On our coaching calls, we'd all agree on strategy and the next steps to move things forward. A week, two weeks, sometimes even a month later, we'd find that little or no progress had been made on the agreed action steps.

Why? Because the business owner was too busy—they were spinning too many plates, putting out fires, and getting distracted by bright, shiny objects. This had become a very common story with many clients.

We tried all the usual "coach" things—accountability, reminders, pushing, etc. Nothing worked because entrepreneurs are typically big-picture, visionary, ideas people. I'm like that, and you may be too. This is a super-important role, but it has one fatal flaw—we're not great at the micro-implementation (more on how to overcome this in Chapter 11).

So we did the next most obvious thing and got them to hire a marketing coordinator. Someone who'd do the day-to-day implementation of the marketing. Stuff that was critical but also stuff that the business owner would find too boring and time-consuming to do consistently.

Then, we hit another roadblock. The entrepreneur would now procrastinate on hiring, take months to get someone on board—and in the end, they often made a bad hire.

We solved this by adding a marketing coordinator recruitment service to the program. We did all the heavy lifting of vetting, hiring, onboarding, and training a marketing coordinator for them. Then we'd work with this person to do the marketing implementation—all the stuff that the entrepreneur couldn't, wouldn't, or hated to do.

Clients started getting massive results. They felt like a big weight had been removed from their shoulders, and they absolutely loved us for doing this for them.

I never imagined we'd be offering a recruitment service when we started coaching and consulting—but here we are. I tapped into existing demand and a strong pain point. It has allowed us to create a world-class program that helps clients get powerful results.

Had I remained in love with my product instead of my clients, I'd still be frustratedly trying to fit a square peg into a round hole.

When the Main Thing Isn't the Main Thing

I've never considered myself a "car guy," but I have several friends who are. One of my closest friends says the car guy is in every man, but it just needs to be awakened. I suspect he's right.

Said friend often ropes me into track days and supercar meetups. There, we risk our lives tearing around racetracks at unreasonable speeds.

The thing I've noticed about Ferrari and other supercar owners is how much joy they get from the sound their cars make. Ferrari engines, especially their V8s and V12s, are renowned for their distinct exhaust notes. Owners and enthusiasts often remark that the sound of their engines is "music to my ears." As someone whose inner car guy is slowly being awakened, I agree.

Many comparatively modest electric cars are actually faster and have much more explosive acceleration than traditional supercars. However, because electric and modern fuel-powered engines run more quietly, they don't give you the same visceral feeling as the thunderous roar of a traditional high-performance engine. It's a bit like sex without the soundtrack. Because of this, some car makers play synthetic engine sounds through the speakers inside the cabin to give the car a perceived feeling of sportiness and ferocity.

Prior to attending supercar gatherings, I would have guessed prospective supercar buyers were mostly interested in speed. And while that's a major selling point, the emotion they feel from the sound is often what seals the deal.

You need to know what your target market is really buying. Often, the main thing you do is relatively undifferentiated and isn't the thing that sways the buying decision.

I came across another example of this recently.

When traveling, many health-conscious people select a hotel by the quality of its fitness facilities. While the hotel's proximity, prices, and room features are factors in the buying decision, these tend to be similar between nearby hotels. The gym is often the deciding factor.

If you own a hotel and don't know that, you might make some costly mistakes. You may spend huge sums of money on refurbishing the rooms in the hopes of attracting more guests when you could have spent a fraction of that upgrading your gym or fitness center. Instead of filling your website with photos of the nearby river and local attractions, which are common to all the other hotels in the area, have detailed photos of the fitness center and an inventory of the workout equipment available.

We frequently conduct in-depth interviews on behalf of our clients to determine why their customers buy from them. Our clients are always surprised by the findings. It's rarely the main thing they do.

Do the Common Thing Uncommonly Well

What does the word "entrepreneur" conjure in your mind? New ideas? Changing the world? Innovation? Venture capital, huge exits?

If you ask the average person who a real entrepreneur is, they might say Steve Jobs, Elon Musk, or Mark Zuckerberg. These are amazing entrepreneurs, for sure, but they're extreme outliers.

Whenever I meet an incredibly wealthy entrepreneur, my curiosity compels me to delve into their success story. It's rare to hear that they came up with a new idea, a revolutionary technology, or some groundbreaking invention. They're usually doing something ordinary and boring. Common answers I've heard recently are "waste management," "a chain of medical clinics," and "a portfolio of e-commerce stores."

Virtually none started with a new idea or concept, and very few raised venture capital or took big risks. They're regular, boring businesses that **do common things uncommonly well.**

Often, these entrepreneurs worked their way up from being employees or running one-person operations to taking over or scaling when the opportunity arose. Their success often came from improving and modernizing processes over five to 20 or more years. Not all heroes wear capes.

Here's a reliable, low-risk path to achieving product-market fit and wealth. Help people get what they already want (the seven core commodities) and reduce the friction it takes them to get it.

Some examples I've recently heard from the owners of these profit machines include:

- Adding an online ordering or booking option

- Integrating with logistics systems of suppliers or customers

- Offering an in-home or delivery service

- Providing the opportunity to rent or lease instead of own

- Customizing a commodity item

- Commoditizing a custom item

- Reducing build or manufacturing time

None of these ideas is revolutionary or requires a genius. People rarely switch suppliers because they get a better product or service. When you reach a certain level of proficiency, there's very little differentiation in the actual thing you do. The switch is often triggered by some existing friction or a perceived reduction of it elsewhere.

I've gone through several accountants in my business career. They all worked with the same tax code and had largely the same bag of tricks for legally minimizing taxes. My switching trigger has never been related to their technical skill or accounting work. It has been things like returning phone calls, being proactive, responding to emails and requests, and so on. In other words, the common things.

Value Killers and Builders

Price and value are the two major variables you'll need to calibrate on your journey to product-market fit. The wider the gap between the perceived value of your product or service and the price, the more demand you'll have.

Everyone wants a great deal. When this gap is sufficiently wide that your market repeatedly says, "Shut up and take my money," is when you truly have product-market fit.

Most entrepreneurs try to widen this gap by lowering their prices, but this is a losing game. In a race to the bottom, the winner gets to go out of business fastest. It's much more powerful to focus on increasing value. Massive value can be unlocked by reducing the friction between your customer and their desired result.

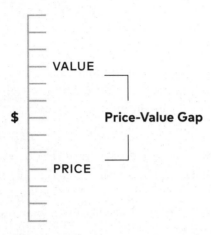

The four major levers that affect the value of what you do are time, effort, risk, and side effects. If these are increased, they impair the value of your product or service. As they are decreased, they enhance your value proposition. These impairments or enhancements may be entirely real or entirely perceived. The result is identical. As far as your prospects are concerned, perception is reality, and perceived value *is* value.

Let's look at each of these value levers.

Time: How long will it take to get the desired result? Pain relief medication that fixes migraines instantly is more valuable than medication that takes three hours to take effect. Some products or services involve an unavoidable time delay, but this can be somewhat mitigated if you can demonstrate some quick wins.

Effort: How easy or hard will it be to get the desired result? If the desired result is a garden shed, one that comes pre-assembled or with an assembly service is more valuable than one that has to be assembled by the purchaser.

Risk: How likely is it that the desired result will be achieved? A medical procedure with a 90 percent chance of success is more valuable than one with a 50 percent chance. The risk lever has two variations—supplier risk and customer risk:

- **Supplier risk:** Will you deliver what you say you will? The best predictor of the future is past performance. This is where reviews, case studies, and testimonials can be powerful proof elements. (I'll discuss these in more detail in Chapter 14.) A risk reversal guarantee can also be helpful, although this still requires trust that you'll actually honor the guarantee.

- **Customer risk:** Will the customer be able to do what you need them to do to get the desired result? Whenever the customer has to do something to get the desired result, a big objection in their mind will be self-doubt. This is a huge sales killer. I may believe that you're an excellent nutritionist, but will I be able to stick to the diet? I may believe that you're an awesome photographer, but am I photogenic enough to get a great headshot?

Side Effects: What will be the negative aspects of getting the desired results? A brand-new car might be the desired result, but having to service and maintain it is a negative side effect. The car is more valuable if servicing and maintenance are included.

The perfect product or service works instantly, takes no effort, is certain to be successful, and has no negative side effects. This would create the most valuable product or service in your category.

The reality is that all products and services are subject to one or more of these value impairments, whether real or perceived. Continuous improvement and the pursuit of perfection are important components of lean thinking. As you decrease the time, effort, risk, and side effects associated with what you do, you'll continue to become more valuable to your market.

Positioning

Years ago, my dad asked me how much money I was making from my business. When I told him, he said, "Ooh, that's even more than a doctor makes!" a doctor being the highest-paid, most prestigious profession he could imagine.

Perhaps it's this childhood conditioning, but whenever I visit a new doctor, I always feel like there's a status standoff where he's trying to signal higher status than me. I say "he" because I never get the same feeling from female doctors.

I recently went to see a specialist. I walk into the aptly named waiting room and check in with the receptionist. "He'll be with you soon," she says, lying to my face. As is usually the case, everything about the experience is designed to optimize his time. The place is adorned with certificates, awards, and honors he has received over the years.

Forty minutes after the scheduled time, my name is finally called, and I enter the doctor's inner sanctum. "Take a seat," he says, without even looking up at me as he flicks through notes in a manila folder with my name on it. His demeanor was one of annoyance, like I was interrupting his day and wasting his time. "What type of work do you do?" he asks, still flicking through the paperwork.

"I'm a marketing consultant and author."

He lowers his glasses, looks me up and down, rolls his eyes, and returns to the paperwork, where he makes a note. I'm pretty sure he wrote "unemployed" in the occupation field. Trying to rescue my fragile ego, I open my mouth to tell him about the bestseller I wrote when he interrupts and says, "OK, take your pants off and lie face down on the table." I don't care how much money you make or how many books you've sold, guy with pants always beats guy with no pants. Well played, Doc. Well played.

I learned two things that day. The first was that a "digital examination" is not done with a computer. The second was the power of positioning. His positioning as a specialist and expert had me tolerate him being late and rude while charging an eye-watering fee for the brief consultation.

I'm by no means suggesting that you use positioning as an excuse for poor customer service. However, premium positioning is absolutely key to being treated and paid well. Right now, you're positioning yourself somewhere in your marketplace. The question is, are you doing so consciously and deliberately?

Most people and businesses position themselves in the mediocre middle. They neither have premium positioning nor are they the cheapest. The middle is crowded and is the worst place to be. Taking an extreme end of the positioning spectrum will give you an instant differentiation advantage.

Choosing to position yourself as the cheapest should be done with extreme caution and only if you have some unique input cost advantage. Otherwise, I recommend avoiding this. You'll attract low-quality customers. These complain the most, pay late, and need the most support. Most of your headaches will come from them.

You might have seen variations of this meme:

$500 Client: "I'm putting my faith in you with this investment and really need you to deliver results."

$50,000 Client: "Wire transfer sent, thanks."

Premium customers also expect results, but there's enough built-in margin to enable you to deliver these. Premium customers also tend to have more realistic expectations. Everyone's had experiences with customers who want to pay nothing but expect everything.

Price and Signaling

In economics, we're taught that price is primarily a function of supply and demand—that people make decisions based on all available information to maximize utility. However, only economists and lunatics believe that people behave rationally. If you've ever seen someone buy a lottery ticket in the hope of getting rich, you know better.

Price is a signal. It can be a signal of quality. If your price is too low, you'll lose quality-seeking customers because they know you can't deliver a high-quality product or service at such a low price.

Price is also a signal of status. If a Rolls-Royce were the price of a Hyundai, it would immediately lose its appeal to the wealthy. Its price is a feature. Part of owning a Rolls-Royce is what it takes to own one.

In our society, humility is idealized in principle but devalued in fact. You may think you're above signaling and status games, but that's unlikely. There'll be some arena where status is important to you, and you need to signal it. Your arena may be wealth, beauty, benevolence, intelligence, fashion, power, or something completely different. Ironically, many go to great lengths to signal humility.

Status signaling may seem wasteful, but it serves a purpose. Signaling is common in the animal kingdom. Animals will engage in irrational and costly behaviors to signal fitness to potential mates or to discourage predators from attacking. Gazelles will sometimes jump high into the air when they spot a predator. This is thought to be a way to signal that they are too healthy and agile to be worth chasing. Peacocks flaunt large, brightly colored tails that are metabolically costly to maintain to signal their fitness to potential mates. Humans do the same thing.

The Utility-Signaling Spectrum

Every product you buy or sell falls somewhere on a spectrum between its intrinsic utility and its value as a signaling device. A $5 T-shirt is primarily utility. A $200 designer T-shirt is primarily signaling.

A college degree exists on this spectrum. There's the utility of knowledge you get, but you could attain that without years on campus and mountains of student debt. In fact, many colleges have their entire curriculum and lectures available online for free. A degree from a prestigious university is mostly about signaling status, competitiveness, and affluence.

In my neighborhood, many homes have a tennis court that's visible from the street. I'm an avid walker, and in the decade I've lived here, I've never once seen anyone playing tennis. A private tennis court is primarily about signaling, not tennis.

Luxury goods raise the status of insiders. Outsiders don't understand why anyone would pay so much for something so ridiculous, and that's the point. It's a similar dynamic to an inside joke. Outsiders don't get it, while insiders feel part of a shared experience.

Over the years, I've had several clients in the diamond business. Almost all of them complained that their products were better quality and cost less than Tiffany diamonds. But they were missing the point. When you say you bought it at Tiffany, or when you open that little robin's-egg blue box, you're not really buying a diamond. You're buying what that means. In fact, a few years ago, Tiffany & Co. was selling an ordinary paper clip for $165 and a gold version for $1,500. Clearly, the buyer is not buying the utility of the paper clip but the story behind it.

If you sell paper clips, it's not enough for you to just mark up the price to $165. Tiffany & Co. has earned its premium positioning and pricing, and you need to do the same.

The Utility-Signaling Spectrum

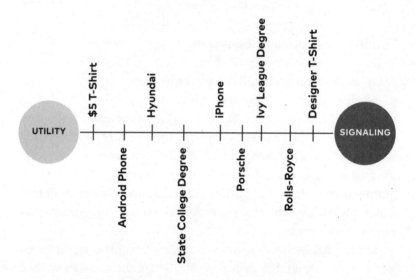

A common mistake is setting prices with a cost-plus pricing model. Cost-plus pricing, or markup pricing, involves calculating input costs and applying a markup percentage to reach an asking price. Customers don't care about your cost structure. A better approach is value-based pricing, where you price your product or service based on the value delivered to customers and the positioning you want in the marketplace.

The Velvet Rope

A DJ wearing oversized headphones sways while fiddling with switches, knobs, and turntables. Cool-looking dudes are surrounded by beautiful women who pulsate to the beat of the music. A red velvet rope segregates this VIP area from the rest, clearly delineating who's in and who's out.

The velvet rope is everywhere, from flying on an airline to attending a concert or visiting an amusement park. It raises the status of the insiders and gives outsiders something to aspire to. A customer who feels like an insider of an exclusive club is more likely to become a raving fan than just a transactional customer. Raving fans are far more valuable to your business.

You can create a velvet rope experience through visual elements, jargon, or insider rituals. I'll share a few examples.

People texting each other on iPhones get blue text message bubbles while everyone else gets green ones. Millions of iPhones have been sold to everyone from bankers to broke students because they didn't want to suffer the indignity of being the only one in their texting peer group with a green bubble.

The washed-out sweater from your college alma mater is another example. It creates an instant connection, and there's a shared insider experience that includes jargon, symbols, mascots, and songs.

Jargon is an important part of signaling insider status. For example, in golf, "breaking 80" is a significant milestone and a symbol of consistent skill for amateur golfers.

A few years ago, I bought a Jeep Wrangler for whenever I needed to transport bicycles, beach gear, or my dog. It's a very poor-quality car, but it's fun and versatile. Whenever I'd pass another Jeep Wrangler, the driver would wave at me. At first, I thought it was someone

I knew and kept trying to recognize these long-lost friends. But then I worked out this was a Jeep Wrangler insider tradition.

The ultimate raving fan is one who associates your brand with their identity.

Various celebrities even have names for their superfans, like Taylor Swift's "Swifties" or Lady Gaga's "Little Monsters."

Use the velvet rope to create an experience that turns your customers or a segment of them into insiders and raises their status.

Chapter 3 Action Items

- What are your customers *really* buying? Use the seven core commodities to understand what is actually motivating your customer to buy.

- Use the four major levers to increase the value of your offer.

- Create a "velvet rope" experience that raises the status of your customers and makes them insiders.

FORCE MULTIPLIER 1

TOOLS

The Right Tool

A while ago, I ordered a large, motorized sit/stand desk for my home office. Unexpectedly, it arrived flat-packed. I tore open the cardboard box, and there lay what seemed like a million pieces packaged in plastic wrapping and polystyrene foam. There were screws of every conceivable size, cables, electrical parts, and an instruction manual that looked like the blueprint for a Boeing 747. It was clearly the handiwork of a disgruntled, sadistic ex-IKEA engineer.

"Shall I call a handyman to assemble it?" my wife asks. Feeling my masculinity challenged, I assure her I can easily handle it.

After several hours of trying to force screws into a metal frame with a rusty old screwdriver, I had bleeding hands and a partially assembled desk.

The fact that I didn't take to it with a sledgehammer right then and there is clear evidence that my anger management training is working. Defeated, I made the call no man wants to make. The handyman arrived a few hours later and confidently opened his toolbox.

I felt like a fool as I watched the screws smoothly glide in with the help of his power drill. He did in minutes what I struggled with for hours.

"Right tool for the right job," I thought, trying to console myself. I've felt similarly stupid manually struggling through some marketing process when a simple tool was available to do it in a fraction of the time.

Becoming Iron Man

Back in the day, humans had to farm by hand. It was back-breaking labor in the fields. When combine harvesters came along, they became one of the most economically important inventions ever, significantly reducing the labor needed to run a farm. Today's agricultural equipment allows one farmer to farm thousands of acres. The unit of output per farmer is now orders of magnitude more than what it was just 150 years ago. This produces far more food for way more people at much lower prices. It created massive leverage for farmers.

LEAN MARKETING PRINCIPLE 4:
Use tools and technology to do the heavy lifting and reduce friction

When used strategically, tools can be the best employee you'll ever have. While you sleep, spend time with family, or do creative work, they keep working on all the tedious and repetitive (but important) tasks in your business. They don't take vacations, and they don't call in sick. More importantly, they can do much of the heavy lifting for you and help you automate, augment, and amplify your marketing processes. Automation does for your time what compound interest does for your money.

Some people take this to mean that technology can take over the entire sales or marketing function. They ask things like, "How do I automate all of my sales?" or "How do I create a funnel that does all the marketing for me?"

While tools can be incredibly powerful, it's easy to get faked out by them. You get faked out because you think if only you had Michelangelo's hammer and chisel, you could create the statue of David as he did.

I often see someone with little grasp of the fundamentals of marketing hoping that some new AI tool or the latest funnel blah-di-blah will solve all their marketing problems. It won't. Tools are important for sure, but how you use them is much more so.

Every good marketing infrastructure is highly process-driven. Some processes will be done with software tools and automation, some will be done by your team, and some will be done with a combination of both. (I'll talk much more about this in the Processes part of this book.)

While your marketing tools might enable you to completely automate many processes, most tools will be used for augmentation rather than complete automation.

A core principle in the Toyota Production System and lean manufacturing is *jidoka*, sometimes called autonomation. *Jidoka* can be roughly translated from Japanese as "automation with a human touch." It blends the strengths of machines (consistency, speed, tirelessness) with the strengths of human workers (judgment, adaptability, insights) to create a more effective and efficient system.

If you've ever watched any of the Iron Man movies, you'll know the character Tony Stark. He's a geeky scientist who uses a powered exoskeletal suit to gain superpowers, which turn him into Iron Man.

In many ways, the suit has the characteristics of autonomation. It blends Stark's intuition, decision-making, and physical actions with the suit's technology, giving him superhuman capabilities. The suit relies on his decision-making and piloting but augments Stark's abilities, enabling him to do far more than he ever could on his own.

A factory starts with the tools and machinery to manufacture products that meet specifications. Similarly, we'll need to start our customer-generating factory with appropriate tooling.

Use Technology to Eliminate Friction

Using tools and technology to remove friction can be a powerful competitive advantage.

It's why you switched to on-demand media streaming and use apps that deliver your food or give you a ride somewhere with a few taps.

Some businesses *create* unnecessary friction with technology. If you've ever hung up in frustration on a telephone voice assistant or abandoned a website because it was too difficult to navigate, you've felt what it's like to be on the receiving end of this.

Rather than alienating and frustrating customers, **lean marketers use tools and technology to do more and better.**

Using tools and technology to do the heavy lifting in your marketing infrastructure and to reduce friction between your customer and their desired result will set you up for rapid growth. So, don the Iron Man suit and become a marketing superhero. 🚀

4

Your Marketing
Nerve Center

CHAPTER 4 SUMMARY

A customer relationship management (CRM) system is the nerve center of your marketing infrastructure. CRM systems help drive and automate many of your marketing, sales, and operational processes.

Highlights covered in this chapter include:

- The three types of CRM systems you need to consider

- The five essential functions you need from your marketing CRM system

- How to tag and segment so that you send highly targeted and relevant messages

- How to use marketing automations and triggers to do the heavy lifting for you

- How to use broadcast messages for time-sensitive communications

- Whether or not you need multiple CRM systems

- How to overcome the challenges of integrating multiple CRM systems

The Best CRM System

Your customer relationship management (CRM) system is the beating heart of your marketing infrastructure.

Used correctly, it will help you drive almost every important process in your business, including lead flow, sales, onboarding, and much more.

Unfortunately, most businesses don't use their CRM system strategically. Most use it purely as a passive database. This data is valuable, but only if it's used to drive action. If you don't do anything useful with your data, you may as well just have it sitting in a spreadsheet (and many businesses do!).

There are three common classes of CRM systems you should be aware of:

- Marketing automation

- Sales management

- Operational

There's usually some overlap in functionality between the three types. Depending on your business, you may need to run one, two, or even all three.

I'm often asked what the "best" CRM system is. The best CRM system is the one that you'll actually use. In the following, I'll discuss each class of CRM system and also point you to some specific recommendations.

Your Marketing Automation CRM System

Marketing CRM systems differ dramatically in price, functionality, and ease of use. There are five basic functions you need them to perform. These are:

- Storing customer data

- Tagging and segmentation

- Triggering automations

- Sending broadcast messages

- Reporting

Any marketing CRM system worth its salt will have all these functions built in, though it may have slightly different terminology for them.

It's also worth noting that while a CRM system may have all these functions, it may be stronger or weaker in one function versus another. This is totally normal. You should choose a CRM system based on which strengths align best with your requirements.

For example, you may have a primarily online business where you use a lot of complex automations, but you only have basic reporting requirements. Or you may have a local brick-and-mortar business, where broadcast message functionality is essential but rudimentary tagging and segmentation are sufficient.

NOTE: In the following sections, I'll talk about "messages" being sent from or triggered by your CRM system. For the purposes of clarity, a "message" can be almost any type of communication. Commonly, it's an email, but it can also be a text message, a push notification, a voice message, or even a postcard or letter sent by mail. Most CRM systems have built-in email messaging functionality and often integrate with third-party services for other types of messages.

Of course, software isn't static. Most CRM software vendors add and improve functionality over time, so once you learn and understand these functions with one system, many of them will easily translate to others.

Let's look at each of these functions in a bit more detail.

Storing Customer Data

The first and most obvious thing a CRM system does is store data about your prospects, leads, and customers. However, this function can vary dramatically in size and scope.

In its most basic form, the system just collects and stores names and email addresses. This may be sufficient if you're a purely digital business with simple requirements. However, most businesses will want to store more data about their prospects, leads, and customers. Some common types of data that you may store in your marketing CRM include:

- Email address

- Physical or mailing address

- Phone or mobile number

- Location information

- Notes and comments

- Birthday or special dates

- Interests

- Actions

Most CRM systems will also allow you to create custom fields so that you can collect a specific type of data that may be important to your business. For example, if you're a florist, collecting the name of your customer's significant other may be important to your business. You might create a custom field in your CRM system called "Partner's Name."

Some of the data in your CRM system may be entered manually, while others will be automatically populated. For example, a good marketing CRM system interfaces directly with your website. This allows it to automatically track the web pages your customers or prospects have visited. While we don't want to be overly creepy in our use of data, such information can be incredibly useful in driving marketing and sales efforts.

Perhaps you're a financial planner and notice that a prospect has visited all the pages on your website related to conservative investments and risk management. This would be useful information when you meet with them or speak to them on the phone. You might steer the conversation in that direction rather than freaking them out with talk of generating large returns with high-risk investments.

You may also wish to enter manual data into your CRM. For example, keeping notes on your discussions with prospects.

Tagging and Segmentation

Sending irrelevant content to your audience is the fastest way to get them to unplug, unsubscribe, or ignore you. It's also costly because you're paying for media that will be wasted. Tags allow you to segment your list in a multidimensional way.

For example, imagine you're a realtor in the idyllic town of Fakeville. Brian, Jenny, and David are in your CRM system. Brian and his family are looking for a holiday home right on the beautiful Fakeville beach. Jenny already lives in Fakeville. Her business has been growing, and she's now looking to upgrade. She loves both the beach and the forest areas, so she's open to either. David doesn't live in the area. He's an investor looking for properties with high rental yields. He's identified Fakeville as one of the towns that meet his investment criteria.

So you have Brian in your CRM system tagged with "holidayhome" and "beach," Jenny tagged with "owneroccupier," "beach" and "forest," and David tagged with "investor" and "yield."

A beautiful new beach house comes on to the market. It's a highend property, but its rental yield would be low. You pull a list of everyone in your CRM system with the "beach" tag. This way, you can send a relevant message to both Brian and Jenny without bothering David.

Later on, a unique property in the forest area is listed. It's been a popular short-term rental property over the last year and has returned the owner market rentals far above average. You pull up a list from your CRM system of everyone with the "forest" or "yield" tags. That way, Jenny and David can be alerted, and Brian won't receive an irrelevant message.

You find out that the government plans to upgrade some key infrastructure in Fakeville. You want to run an information session for investors to show them how this will create more employment in the town and a much higher demand for housing. You pull up a list of people with an "investor" tag. David would get a relevant, time-sensitive message, while Brian and Jenny would be excluded.

This is a very simple example, but it illustrates how to use tags to be highly relevant and targeted. If you had sent every message to everyone on the list, they would all have received a lot of irrelevant, possibly annoying messages; such messages create marketing "waste" because they damage your connection with your audience and create no value for them. Tagging and segmenting allow you to send the right message to the right people at the right time.

A good rule of thumb is to over-tag rather than under-tag. Perhaps you sell online only and don't see any need to tag people by geographic location. It's better to over-tag and have that data available than be hamstrung by its absence later. If you want to open your first brick-and-mortar location five years from now, having everyone's location data on your list would be incredibly useful.

Triggering Automations

Automations are a highly underrated and underused feature of CRM systems. Once you start using them, you'll never know how you lived without them. They can do a lot of the heavy lifting for you.

Automations can be triggered by many factors, such as user behavior, elapsed time, tags, and an almost unlimited number of variables. They are limited only by your imagination.

For example, adding someone to your CRM system could trigger a welcome sequence. Your sequence might include a welcome email that goes out immediately. Then, 24 hours later, a task is created for one of your salespeople to give them a call. Following that, 48 hours later, an educational email may be sent. This is an example that uses time-based triggers. I'll go into more detail on welcome sequences and email marketing in Chapter 12.

You might get a bit more sophisticated and start introducing behavior-based triggers. For example, if a prospect views pricing information for a particular product on your website, your CRM system could trigger an automation that sends them targeted emails based on that product.

You've likely seen "abandoned cart" automations. You've added a product or two to your cart on an e-commerce store but didn't finish the checkout process. An hour or two later, you get an email reminding you that you have items remaining in your cart with a helpful link or discount code to encourage you to complete your order. That's an example of a behavior-based automation. They are very effective and will instantly boost sales and rescue revenue that would have otherwise been lost.

Sending Broadcast Messages

Broadcast messages are ideal for time-sensitive communications. They are typically manually sent or scheduled for a particular date and time.

Take the case of a Black Friday campaign. You might send a post-card in the mail to your VIP customers with a discount code a week ahead of time so they can get in first before you sell out. Before and during the Black Friday sale, you might build excitement and fear of missing out with emails to your list. Finally, a few hours before Black Friday ends, you might send a "last chance" text message. Using multiple mediums is a powerful way to get more attention and mindshare with your audience.

If your content is mostly evergreen, you might rely on auto-mations for lead nurturing. For example, if you teach yoga, your content will be relevant today, a year from now, and probably many years from now. You can reuse this content very efficiently.

However, if your content is time-bound or "perishable," you'll use mostly broadcast messages. For example, a realtor sending alerts about new listings coming on to the market is sharing content that's relevant right now but will be obsolete soon.

Reporting

There's a lot going on in your marketing CRM system, so it's an important data source for determining the effectiveness of your marketing.

We want our system to tell us basic things like who opened a message, how many clicked the "buy" button, and how many followed through and completed the purchase.

Reporting can also get much more sophisticated. Some CRM systems have lead-scoring functionality. They may score each contact in your CRM system based on their behavior. If a lead opens all of your emails, clicks on links, and spends a lot of time browsing your website, they're likely much hotter than someone who never opens emails or interacts with your content.

In most cases, you can trigger automations based on lead score changes. For example, if a contact changes from warm to hot, you can trigger an automation that will create a task for one of your sales reps to give them a call.

Some CRM systems track a lot of metrics and produce comprehensive reports. (I'll cover metrics in more detail in Chapter 15.) Others have more basic reporting functionality and require you to export their data to a separate tool to produce the reports you need.

Your Sales Management CRM System

If you have a sales team, you'll likely need a sales management CRM system to manage their activities and sales pipeline.

If your sales process is very basic, you may be able to get away with using your marketing automation CRM system for this purpose. However, most businesses that have a sales team and multiple touchpoints with prospects during their sales cycle will likely need a dedicated sales management CRM system. It can be frustrating to have to run multiple tools that seem similar or have overlapping features. The trade-off between simplicity and specialization is one you'll have to make often when choosing your marketing tools.

A key function of your sales CRM system is to assign and track the activities of each salesperson in your team. Who should they call or email next? Depending on whether you do outbound or inbound sales activities (or a mix of both), you'll likely track different metrics and activities in your system.

Some sales management CRM systems have built-in emailing and calling functionality. Some even allow you to record calls and store the recording inside the system for future coaching and review.

Whether you use a full-blown sales management CRM system or combine it with your marketing automation system, you'll need something to keep track of sales activity and performance.

Your Operational CRM System

Once you start working with a customer, you need a way to keep track of your interactions with them.

Depending on your industry and the type of work you do, the type of operational CRM system you use may differ substantially.

A shared spreadsheet or database may be sufficient if your requirements are extremely basic. However, most businesses outgrow this quickly as their team, customer base, and requirements grow.

If you do project-based work or have a consulting type of business, a project management tool will likely be the best operational CRM system for you. Such businesses include marketing agencies, professional consulting firms, and coaching and training businesses.

If your work is more transactional or break-and-fix related, something like a helpdesk, service, or job management system would be your operational CRM system. This fits trades, construction, telecommunications, and IT businesses well.

If you mostly sell products from an online store or marketplace, your operational CRM system will likely be built into your e-commerce platform.

If you work in a highly regulated industry or one that has specialized workflows, you'll likely use an industry-specific operational CRM system. These usually encompass the compliance and regulatory aspects and are often used by medical practices, financial services firms, mortgage brokers, law firms, and realtors.

In the medical space, practice management systems can store X-rays, manage patient appointments, and securely store clinical notes.

In financial services, there are systems that ensure your advice and recommendations are compliant with legal and regulatory requirements. They may also perform specialized tasks like calculating insurance premiums and generating documents.

Regardless of your industry, your operational CRM system should help you and your team:

- Have up-to-date customer, client, or patient contact information

- Keep notes about interactions with customers, clients, or patients

- Store relevant files or links to files

- Ensure compliance with any regulatory requirements

- Manage and report on the status of workflows, jobs, or projects

Tying Your CRM Systems Together

Your CRM systems will play important roles at different stages of your customer journey.

You'll make heavy use of your marketing automation CRM system in the awareness stage.

There'll likely be some crossover between your marketing automation and sales management CRM systems in the lead nurturing stage as prospects are warmed up and identify themselves as warm or hot leads.

Your sales management system will likely be a key tool in your sales conversion stage.

Your operations CRM system will feature heavily in the delivery phase and will be important in helping you deliver a world-class experience.

While using multiple CRM systems adds complexity to your tool stack, this can be mitigated through inter-system integration. Some systems natively support integration with each other, particularly between marketing automation and sales management systems.

Another way to integrate your CRM systems is with third-party workflow automation tools. These connect your systems and can sync data between them. They also allow you to add useful logic to your integrations.

For example, you might create a workflow that triggers when a prospect in your marketing automation CRM system is identified as a hot lead. This workflow would create a deal in your sales management system and assign a task to a salesperson on your team to contact them. If the deal closes, your sales management CRM system could trigger another workflow to create a customer account in your operational CRM system and start the onboarding process.

Compare marketing CRM systems and find which one is right for you inside the Lean Marketing Hub. Go to LeanMarketing.com/hub

Some CRM systems encompass marketing automation, sales management, and operational components, but it's unusual for them to do all these functions well. This may be a trade-off you're willing to accept in exchange for the simplicity of having a single system.

Another all-in-one approach is using a general CRM system development, customization, and application platform. You can then customize it to your industry or business requirements and build the marketing automation, sales management, and operational functions you need. This is often the approach taken by larger enterprises.

Unless you have a huge budget, an in-house IT department, and a very high tolerance for pain, I'd recommend you avoid this option. I've often seen it turn into a white elephant project with expensive and long-running software development cycles. It also creates a high degree of lock-in with your software developer because of the custom components that need to be created and maintained. The same downsides of all-in-one systems apply here also—it'll likely be a jack of all trades and master of none.

Chapter 4 Action Items

- If you already have a marketing CRM system, evaluate if it's meeting your needs. If you don't already have one, trial a few to see which might be best for you.

- Ensure you're tagging and segmenting the contacts in your CRM system.

- Use your marketing CRM system to automate manual parts of your lead nurturing processes.

5

Programming Moist Robots

CHAPTER 5 SUMMARY

The words you use radically affect the results you get. By becoming better at copywriting, you'll become a better marketer.

Highlights covered in this chapter include:

- How to "program" your target market to do what you want them to do

- The biggest mistake in copywriting and how to avoid it so that you command attention

- The ten copywriting commandments that will help you become more influential and persuasive

- How the wrong words caused a deadly accident and how to avoid this mistake in your marketing

- How to press the emotional buying triggers of your target market

- How to defeat writer's block forever

- The magnetic messaging framework for crafting short-form messages that are compelling and action-oriented

Your Words Make All the Difference

In Chapter 3, I introduced the concept of "moist robots" and the seven core commodities that drive all human behavior.

Just as a computer programmer uses code to make a computer do something, skillful marketers use words to influence people. This chapter is all about writing the "code" that gets moist robots to do what you want them to do.

Marketing is the master skill of business, and copywriting is the master skill of marketing. I hesitated to use the word "copywriting" in this chapter because what we're about to discuss is so much more than that word encompasses.

Learning how to communicate so that others will listen and take action will touch every area of your life. In this chapter, I'll share with you the most powerful technology when it comes to influence and persuasion with words. It's the ultimate tool in your marketing toolbox, and we'll spend some time sharpening it.

A not-so-smart person who can communicate well will always beat a super-smart person who can't. That's great news because it's much easier to upgrade your communication skills than your intelligence.

Phil M. Jones, author of *Exactly What to Say*, has the mantra, "Change your words. Change your world." I couldn't agree more. I've had no better return on time invested in my personal and professional life than learning to use words well. You're here right now because of it.

Copywriting touches every part of marketing, even if you're not "writing." The basic unit of almost anything you do marketing-wise is words, even if they are used in video or audio.

In this chapter, I'll give you my best advice on writing powerful copy that moves your prospects and customers to action.

While I do entertain fantasies of one day writing titillating erotica, for the moment we're going to focus on words that make you money. Making money is a turn-on for many, so maybe I'm hitting two birds with one stone.

Either way, the type of writing I'm focusing on is not the type that will win you a Pulitzer Prize. Your broke, art-for-art's-sake brother-in-law, with a degree in philosophy, won't be impressed with your writing. But your private banker will be. I hope that's OK with you. If not, then now would be a good time to give this book to someone else.

Good copy forms the building blocks of everything I'll discuss in the Assets and Processes parts of this book. To write great marketing copy, follow my ten copywriting commandments.

Copywriting Commandment 1: Thou Shalt Entertain

Whether someone plans to write an email sequence or a sales page or record a video or podcast, a common question is, "How long should it be?" That's kind of like asking, "How many leaves are on a tree?" or "How big is a bowl of nachos?" Let's get one thing straight: a bowl of nachos should always be huge, overflowing with salsa and melted cheese.

When it comes to creating content, there's a common misconception that people have short attention spans. Because of this, you'll hear a lot of nonsense advice like "keep your emails short" or "make your videos 2–3 minutes long." Yet people binge-watch numerous episodes of a Netflix series, finish multi-hour podcasts, and go down YouTube rabbit holes for hours at a time.

The reality is people don't have short attention spans, they have short *boredom* spans. The volume of available content has massively increased, so why would anyone choose a boring option when more entertaining ones exist? If you keep your audience engaged, they will pay attention.

This brings us to the cardinal rule of copywriting: **don't be boring.** You can break almost any other rule except this one.

In fact, a great way to think of your content is as *infotainment.* Yes, we want to inform, educate, motivate, and so on, but your information won't get consumed if it's boring. Think of entertainment as the carrier for your message. If it's not packaged in entertainment, then your message won't get through.

Have you ever been on a busy highway that has slowed to a crawl because of an accident up ahead? It's frustrating. As you approach the scene of the accident, you see the strobing light of an ambulance and realize that the accident is on the opposite side. There's no logical reason for it to be slowing down your side of the highway. Then, the penny drops. You realize it's because each driver ahead of you slows down as they pass by to rubberneck and gawk at the accident on the other side. Righteous indignation kicks in, and you exclaim, "Idiots!" All these nosy people with nothing better to do are why you're now running half an hour late. But guess what happens when you pass by the scene? Of course, you slow down and look, too.

Compelling copy is similar. It hooks into human curiosity, and you simply can't resist it even if, or perhaps especially if, it's not pretty. It's kind of like those "fail" videos on YouTube. They're painful to watch. You know what's going to happen when he climbs that precariously balanced ladder, but of course, you can't look away.

This kind of "can't look away" copy is sometimes referred to by copywriters as a greased slide or slippery slope. In *The Adweek Copywriting Handbook*, legendary copywriter Joseph Sugarman explains it this way:

> Picture a steep slide at a playground. Now picture somebody putting baby oil or grease along the entire length of the slide including the side rails. Picture yourself now climbing up the ladder, sitting at the top of the slide and then letting gravity force you down the slide.

As you start to slide down and build momentum, you try holding on to the sides to stop, but you can't stop. You continue to slide down the slide despite all your efforts to prevent your descent. This is the way your copy must flow.

Every element in an advertisement must cause that slippery slide effect. The headline must be so powerful and compelling that you must read the subheadline, and the subheadline must be so powerful that you are compelled to read the first sentence, and the first sentence must be so easy to read and so compelling that you must read the next sentence and so on, straight through the entire copy to the end.

What if you sell something serious, though? Is it always appropriate to be entertaining? By entertaining, I don't necessarily mean funny. Being inappropriately funny can detract from your message. Your job isn't to be a comedian. Your job is to be compelling enough that people pay attention to you.

Let's take a serious product like business insurance. Which headline grabs your attention and compels you to read more:

Great Prices on Business Insurance

or

What Will You Do When Your Personal Assets Are Seized to Satisfy a Judgment Against Your Corporation?

The world wants you to be vanilla. It wants you to fit into a very safe box. You need to resist this with every fiber of your being.

Being entertaining means that your words are unignorable. So, what exactly does this look like? Like the distinction between art and pornography, it's hard to describe precisely, but you know it when you see it. In the following nine copywriting commandments, I'll do my best to break it down as precisely as possible.

Copywriting Commandment 2:
A Confused Mind Says No

As marketers, we want our target market to respond positively. But if our message is unclear, they'll get confused, and a confused mind says "no." To get people to say "yes," our copy needs to be simple and clear.

Here are some ways to ensure your words are simple and clear.

Write the way you talk. A common copywriting mistake is going into "professional" or "academic" mode. You'll get professional mode when you see police speaking to the media. They might say something like, "Two males were engaged in an altercation, during which time the suspect discharged his weapon and fatally wounded the victim." The same person in a casual situation would simply say, "Two guys were fighting, then one of them pulled out a gun and killed the other guy."

Be intentional with your words. A profound piece of wisdom I heard years ago is that the message sent is not always the same as the message received. I've kept that in mind ever since. Whether I'm speaking to a client, an employee, a supplier, or my family, I'm mindful that they may be receiving a message that's vastly different from the one I'm sending. This insight has made me much more intentional about the words I use. Remember, people respond to and make buying decisions based on what they heard, not on what was said or meant.

Write simple sentences. Chances are, if you can't articulate your message simply, your audience will have trouble understanding it. The best communicators use simple language. Simple language is persuasive. A good way to do this is by not putting multiple thoughts in a single sentence. Long and complicated sentences are confusing and hard to understand.

Cut your way to perfection. Simple means getting rid of extra words. Never say something with ten words when you could do it in eight. Don't use seven sentences when you can get the idea across in three. A lot of writing involves cutting out unneeded words and sentences.

Generally, the more you cut out, the better the writing will be. French mathematician and philosopher Blaise Pascal famously wrote, "If I had more time, I would have written a shorter letter." The most time-consuming part of good writing is editing. Many writers worry about writer's block. I think a worse problem is "writer's diarrhea."

When your Wi-Fi or cell phone drops out or suffers poor performance, it's often because the signal-to-noise ratio is too low. There's not enough signal getting through the noise caused by interference or too many other devices transmitting simultaneously. In copywriting, unneeded words are noise. You want the signal-to-noise ratio of your writing to be high.

We've all been stuck listening to someone, often a politician or company PR person, who speaks a lot of words but doesn't really say anything. Their signal-to-noise ratio is way too low.

Have you ever heard the children's nursery rhyme "Old Mac-Donald Had a Farm"? It uses a lot of words to convey a small number of thoughts. If we were rewriting it with a high signal-to-noise ratio, it would go like this: Old MacDonald had a farm with cows, chickens, and pigs. The end.

Use simple words. Avoid jargon or overly academic or complex language. Use words with only one or two syllables. A good rule of thumb is, would a 12-year-old understand what you're talking about? There are simple apps you can use to grade the difficulty level of your writing.

Make your text visually easy. Use paragraphs that only have a few sentences. Big, long slabs of text are hard on the eye. Break your text up with paragraphs, bullet points, and subheadings (more on this last point in Commandment 9).

Write drunk, edit sober. Don't try to write and edit at the same time. Writing and editing are two different modes. When writing, just get all your ideas out on the page, even if you're embarrassed by the result (and you will be). Take an hour break or do something else, then edit. If you're writing something longer, editing on a different day can be very helpful to see your work with fresh eyes.

I'll leave you with one final pro hack I use to ensure I write clearly. As part of your final edit, get your computer to speak back your text. Most operating systems have text-to-speech functionality built in.

When you read your own writing, you interpret it with the same brain that created it. Often, this makes you read what you meant to write or thought you wrote rather than what's actually on the page. When your computer reads back verbatim what you've written, it's very unforgiving. This makes any weird sentence structures or overly long and confusing sentences much more apparent.

Copywriting Commandment 3: Thou Shalt Write Awesome Headlines

Legendary adman David Ogilvy said: "On the average, five times as many people read the headline as read the body copy. When you have written your headline, you have spent 80 cents out of your dollar."

If 80 percent of people aren't reading past your headline, here's an easy way to visualize what's happening. Imagine five people standing in front of you while you talk. Four of them will turn and walk away after your first sentence. One person stays and listens to the rest of what you have to say. If you knew that would be the case, wouldn't you be much more thoughtful and deliberate about that first sentence?

However, writers usually spend most of their time writing the body copy and a tiny fraction on the headline. See the mismatch?

You should front-load your copywriting efforts because if the headline doesn't hook them, they won't ever see the rest.

"Headline" can mean a literal headline, like for a sales letter or article, or it can be whatever the equivalent of a headline is for the content you're creating. For example, on YouTube, this would be your video's thumbnail image and title. On a podcast, it would be the title of the episode. On a short-form social media video, it would be your hook in the first few seconds of the video.

A good copywriter will spend significant time on the headline. If you're going to spend an hour writing something, I recommend spending at least 15 of those 60 minutes on writing headlines and subheadlines. Aim for at least 50 variations. This feels strange and over the top, but it's very effective.

A trick used by journalists for a long time to create attention-grabbing headlines is to make an extreme or unusual claim but frame it as a question. For example, "Could This Be the Cure for Cancer?" By presenting it as a question, they draw attention to the implied claim without accountability for its veracity.

If the writer was confident that this really was a cancer cure, they would have made the headline an assertion like "Cure for Cancer Found!" This is so prevalent in journalism that Betteridge's law of headlines states, "Any headline that ends in a question mark can be answered by the word No." While a little sneaky, the question style can be a useful tool to help juice up your headlines.

Your headline must grab them, entertain them, and suck them into the first sentence. I recently came across this headline in my news feed:

> How One Very Lucky Enron Exec Made $280 Million by Impregnating a Stripper, Destroying His Marriage, and Losing His Job

Here's a classic headline and subheadline from the *Northern Territory News*, a newspaper in Australia that's notorious for its crazy stories:

> **Why I Stuck a Cracker Up My Clacker**
> A man who suffered serious burns when friends lit a firecracker in his bum says he was just showing his visiting mates a Territory good time.

(As if the headline wasn't compelling enough, the accompanying photo is of a guy drinking beer with a snake wrapped around the beer bottle!)

Just like you get mad at those rubbernecking drivers, you're probably thinking, "Who reads this crap?" Well, I checked your browsing history, and it turns out you do.

Of course, these are extreme examples, but if 80 cents out of your dollar is spent on the headline, you need to make sure it's doing its job.

Copywriting Commandment 4: Name It and Claim It

A rose by any other name would smell as sweet... but it wouldn't sell anywhere near as well. If a rose was called a Prickly Stemmed Fungal Fuchsia, I doubt it would be the bestselling flower it is today, despite being functionally the same.

Ever notice how famous actors have such cool-sounding names like Tom Cruise, Vin Diesel, and Whoopi Goldberg? It's no accident. Many have changed their names or adopted stage names to align with their personal brand. Tom was originally Thomas Mapother, Vin was Mark Sinclair, and Whoopi was Caryn Johnson. Many actors change their names when they join the Screen Actors Guild.

Similarly, companies and products sometimes need a little reboot. A great example of this is the so-called vegan leather used in Tesla car interiors. Of course, vinyl or plastic, which is what it is, doesn't fit Tesla's positioning as being luxurious or environmentally friendly—but "vegan leather" is much more like it.

Maybe we could do the same for the rhinoceros, some species of which are critically endangered. They have a terrible name that's hard to pronounce, hard to spell, and certainly doesn't evoke a warm and cuddly vibe. How about "chubby unicorn"?

Blue Ribbon Sports became Nike (after the Greek goddess of victory). When fried foods started gaining a reputation for being unhealthy, Kentucky Fried Chicken changed to KFC.

Name and claim your key frameworks, processes, or products. This is important for positioning, branding, and intellectual property protection. In Chapter 10, I'll discuss intellectual property and the more technical aspects of naming.

I certainly didn't invent marketing, but I named and claimed my key frameworks and processes like the 1-Page Marketing Plan and Lean Marketing. These have become my best-known brands, arguably more important than my own name.

Copywriting Commandment 5: Ask and You Shall Receive

Avianca Flight 52 was a regularly scheduled flight from Bogotá, Colombia, to New York City. On January 25, 1990, the Boeing 707 ran out of fuel and crashed 20 miles short of John F. Kennedy International Airport. Eight of the nine crew members and 65 of the 149 passengers on board were killed.

The natural question arises: How does a plane run out of fuel just short of its destination airport? A fuel leak? Some technical fault? It was neither of those things for Avianca Flight 52.

Due to weather conditions, the aircraft had been kept in a holding pattern around JFK. The flight had previously been given two delay estimates that had already passed. By then, they had been in their holding pattern, waiting for permission to land, for so long that they had serious concerns about their fuel levels.

At that point, first officer Mauricio Klotz radioed the air traffic controller, saying, "Ah well I think we need priority." Then in various subsequent communications, he said things like, "Ah we'll try once again we're running out of fuel," and, "Yes sir ah we'll be able to hold about five minutes that's all we can do."

To you or me, in hindsight, these messages may sound alarming. However, to the air traffic controller simultaneously managing dozens of delayed flights in poor weather with lots of back-and-forth communications going on, these ambiguous messages easily got lost in the background.

Air traffic controllers are trained to immediately respond to very specific words like "Mayday," "pan-pan," and "emergency," none of which was ever uttered by the crew of Avianca Flight 52. Sadly, this sealed its fate and unnecessarily cost many lives.

While this is an extreme example, it highlights the dangers of timidity and the importance of clear and direct language when you need to make something happen.

I see a lot of websites, emails, and marketing material that do many things right but are timid when asking for action. You need to lead your audience and tell them exactly what you want them to do. "Click Here," "Get Started," "Download Now," and "Reply to This Email" are some good examples.

Much of this timidity comes from the common misconception that marketing is about "awareness." Awareness is great, but there's a world of difference between awareness and action.

You're aware that Switzerland is a country. But that doesn't mean you have plans to travel there.

You're aware that vegetables are good for you. But that doesn't mean you're going to have them for dinner.

In marketing, awareness is a good start, but action is what you really want.

One writer of ancient times said, "Ask and you shall receive." To get more of what you want in life and business, you must become a good asker. Asking is the beginning of the receiving process. If you find you're not getting enough of what you want, failure to ask clearly and directly might be your problem.

Copywriting Commandment 6: Emotion Commits the Crime, Logic Does the Cover-Up

One thing you must know if you're going to successfully "program" moist robots is that they run on emotion, not logic. They may pretend to run on logic, but for the most part, you'll get nowhere with them if you rely on logic alone.

Since my dad's passing, I think about him every day. What I miss most were his little "dad jokes" and often inappropriate "observations." He'd find them funnier than any of us did, but his laughter at his own hilarity was contagious and always got us laughing too.

He certainly wasn't a model of modern woke correctness, but it was never mean-spirited.

Once, we were at McDonald's, which was a special treat for us back then. As we approached the front of the queue, he elbowed me and motioned with his eyebrows at a portly fellow ahead of us in line. Then he whispered, "He ordered two Big Macs, a large fries, and... get this...," trying to hold back a giggle, "a *Diet* Coke."

This was ironic given that Dad was quite overweight for most of his life, but I guess he felt he was more honest about why he was there. When we came to the front of the line, he placed our order and winked at me as he emphasized to the server, "and a *regular* Coke." The eye rolls from us ensued.

Take what you will from that anecdote, but it is instructive that ever since McDonald's introduced their "healthy menu" featuring salads and vegetables, sales of their classic menu items like the Big Mac and fries have skyrocketed.

The "healthy menu" made going to McDonald's not necessarily a guilt-inducing run for junk food. You *could* be ordering a kale salad, though their sales data tells us you won't be. Emotion commits the crime, and logic does the cover-up.

A lot of what we do as marketers is understand and tap into people's irrational behavior. Many of my early marketing efforts failed miserably because, being geeky and analytical by nature, I tried to use logic, facts, and features and benefits in my copy. I eventually learned that people buy primarily with emotions and justify with logic. Logic must be smuggled in under the cover of darkness while the fireworks of emotion provide the perfect diversion.

I've heard some pushback on this from people who sell technical products or business-to-business (B2B). "That works with consumers, but I'm selling to CEOs" is a common objection.

You're not selling to CEOs, nor are you selling B2B or B2C—these are all conceptual designations. You're selling H2H: human-to-human. And humans buy with emotion first and justify with logic later whether they're the CEO or the janitor.

The slogan "Nobody ever got fired for buying IBM" sold billions of dollars worth of equipment to C-suite executives all over the world. This is a great example of emotion-driven buying behavior by sophisticated buyers. As someone who came from deep in the underbelly of the IT industry, I can tell you firsthand that IBM has never been the cheapest, best-performing, or best-value option. It's a completely irrational choice—until you realize how buying is really done.

Optics are extremely important in B2B and enterprise sales. Almost everyone from the CEO down is thinking, "Will this make me look stupid to my boss or get me fired?" In B2B and enterprise sales, presenting yourself as the "safe" option will get you far further than presenting yourself as the best or most innovative one. In the corporate world, you'll rarely get praised or promoted for making an optimal buying decision, but you will face negative consequences for making a bad one.

Sophisticated C-suite executives are the same emotion-fueled moist robots who order two Big Macs, a large fries, and a Diet Coke, or click on sensational clickbait headlines. Their occupation doesn't make them any less susceptible to making decisions with emotion.

Here are two ways to implement this in your copy.

1. When writing, start with the emotion. What's the emotion you want your audience to feel? Tap into the seven core commodities. What are they really buying? Do they want status? Wealth? Freedom? It will likely be a combination of multiple core commodities, but there may be one dominant one.

You can still include the logical stuff like pricing, value, specifications, and so on. But know that their main role is to justify the purchase after the fact. To do the cover-up, if you will.

Part of the logic in your copy will likely be numbers and statistics. These get boring fast and should be considered a copywriting danger zone. You will likely lose your readers if these are voluminous or complex, so careful thought needs to be given to how you present them.

2. Make numbers mean something. Don't just say, "five gigabytes of hard drive storage." Say, "1,000 songs in your pocket." Don't just say, "We have 3 million subscribers." Say, "If our subscriber base were a city, we'd be the third-largest city in America." See how much more compelling that is?

Copywriting Commandment 7: Write Before You Write

We've all experienced page fright—helplessly staring at a blank screen as the cursor flips you off with every blink. This is a very real problem if you start writing when you start writing.

I think about writing more as filling in the blanks than creating something right there on the spot.

I once heard Seth Godin say there's no such thing as writer's block and that you never hear of a plumber with plumber's block. I agree. A professional plumber who attends a job arrives with tools in hand. A copywriter should, too.

I make sure I'm never stumped, staring at a blinking cursor or blank page when it's time to write, by having my toolbox handy. Here's the bag of tricks I use to keep the words flowing:

Story bank: I'll cover the importance of storytelling in Commandment 8. Having a bank of interesting stories on hand that you can draw from will make your writing better and more memorable.

Content bank: I keep a file of "best of" ideas. When I think of, hear, read, or see an interesting idea, I note it down in my content file. I have sections in my content file for various topics of interest to me, like marketing, sales, influence, success, and so on. Then, when I need to write or create something, I've got awesome ideas to draw on.

Swipe file: See a great ad, headline, email, or sales page? Keep a copy in your swipe file to use as inspiration and to spark ideas when you're writing your own.

Snippets: These are verbatim phrases, sentences, and paragraphs. When I hear or read something phrased in an interesting or unique way, I add it to my snippets file. It's similar to the swipe file but on a more micro level. I use this as inspiration for my own writing.

"Made me buy": If I clicked on an ad or email or saw something else that made me buy, I keep a screenshot or copy. It's great inspiration for when I'm crafting a campaign.

You can organize these any way you like, but I've found it easiest to just have them as free-form notes that I can access, search, and add to on all my devices.

I've compared my process with professional authors, and they all have a pretty similar set of tools.

The only downside is that being a passive listener or reader becomes virtually impossible. You'll always be pausing videos, podcasts, or your reading because you want to add something to one of your files.

Copywriting Commandment 8: Tell Stories

Humans are hardwired to receive messages using stories. This predates the written word by many thousands of years. Stories take up storage space in people's heads. You'll remember a story someone told long after you've forgotten the main thing they were talking about.

Whether it's that movie that never fails to make you laugh no matter how many times you've watched it (*Office Space* for me) or the novel that made you ugly-cry, we're all moved by stories.

Stories entertain, make your message much stickier, and, most importantly, move people emotionally, which puts them in the buying zone.

There are many storytelling frameworks. The "hero's journey" is a well-known one often used for longer-form content. The more complex the framework, the less likely you are to use it. Here's a super-simple, two-step framework for storytelling, which I learned from Vinh Giang, an amazing storyteller and showman:

1. The incident. The who, what, where, and when. Relive the story rather than just reporting it. The difference between reporting and reliving is VAKS (visual, auditory, kinesthetic, smell). This is how you add color to the story and bring it to life.

Reporting is "I almost missed the bus." Reliving is "I was pummeled by the ice-cold rain as I sprinted through the dimly lit streets. Out of breath and exhausted, I reached the bus stop just as the bus pulled up."

2. The point. This turns information into insight and makes the story relevant. "The reason I'm telling you this is because..." Leave the point to the end of the story. This way, you can link almost any story to any situation or point.

Analogies, metaphors, and similes are also very powerful storytelling devices at a more micro level. "He dealt with enemies as a cleaver deals with meat" is more vivid and memorable than "He was ruthless."

A story is a bazooka, whereas an analogy, metaphor, or simile is like a handgun. (There, I did it again.) Analogies simplify the complex, connect the unknown to the known, and add fun and life to your copy. They make people say or think, "I never thought about it that way," and are a great rapport-building device.

Tap into your library of stories. As discussed in Commandment 7, build a story bank. Document anything that moves you, intrigues you, makes you laugh, or makes you cry.

Copywriting Commandment 9: Create a Dual Readership Path

Some people are readers, some are skimmers, and most are a combination of both. Regular subheadlines allow readers to take everything in while skimmers still get the gist of your content. This creates a dual readership path.

Throughout this book, I've broken up chapters and long blocks of text with regular subheadings. This is easier on the eyes, entices skimmers back into the main copy, and allows sections to be more self-contained.

A dual readership path is not just for text-based content. For example, on most audio and video platforms like YouTube or podcasts, you can use chapter markings to break up your content, allowing viewers or listeners to quickly navigate to segments of an episode and easily know what else is coming up.

A dual readership path is a great way to retain your audience's attention.

Copywriting Commandment 10: Summarize Before and After

Notice how each chapter of this book begins with a short summary and highlights of what's coming up? This is kind of like a preview of coming attractions. Also, at the end of every chapter, there are action items that remind you of the main points and help you turn information into action.

These elements, along with the regular subheadings, make the book easier to follow and return to.

Whenever you're writing or speaking, first **tell them what you're going to tell them.** This opens a loop and is a great way to capture and retain their attention. Afterward, **tell them what you just told them.** This helps with retention and comprehension. Finally, provide practical action items based on what you just taught to help them get tangible results.

Change Your Words, Change Your World

These ten copywriting commandments are not an exhaustive list of what will make you an excellent copywriter and communicator, but they'll give you 80 percent of the results for 20 percent of the effort.

If you want to go deeper into writing advice, I recommend two books. The first is *The Elements of Style* by William Strunk Jr. and E.B. White. It's a short book with principles that have stood the test of time. I reread it every few years. The second is *On Writing* by Stephen King. This is an excellent book that's easy and entertaining to read and has solid advice from a master of the craft.

If you change your words, you'll change your world and the results you get. Implement these ten copywriting commandments in your business and your life. Having a salary negotiation with your boss? Make your impressive numbers mean something. Trying to get your kids to eat their vegetables? Tell them a story and connect it to something important to them. Want your prospects to respond to your marketing campaign? Tell them exactly what to do in a clear, direct manner.

The Magnetic Messaging Framework

Now that we've covered some broader aspects of copywriting, I want to give you a simple framework for crafting shorter-form, stand-alone messages. These shorter-form messages might be used in ads, landing pages, the top fold of your website, or anywhere else you need to attract the reader's attention and compel them to take action.

With longer-form copy, you have the luxury of time and space to explain things; however, with shorter-form copy, every word must earn its keep. Unnecessary words should be viewed as obstacles to the impact of your message. Like a data compression algorithm, you want to squeeze a lot of information and meaning into a small amount of space.

There are seven filters that I pass messages through to ensure they're magnetic. While it's unlikely that you'll hit every single one in a short-form message, you want to try hard to hit as many of them as possible. These filters are:

1. Is it about them? So many messages on websites, emails, and ads are self-focused. You'll commonly see self-aggrandizing state-ments like "We deliver best-of-breed products," "We were founded in 1985," and so on. No one cares. Everybody's concerned about themselves and their problems. If your message is too self-focused, it will fall on deaf ears. Have you ever been stuck with someone who keeps talking about themselves? It's like being socially water-boarded. Your prospects feel the same way. So, make your message about the prospect and the problem they're experiencing.

2. Is it easy to understand? As per Copywriting Commandment 2, always prioritize clarity. Sometimes, it can be tempting to be witty or clever in shorter-form messages. That's fine, but it should never compromise clarity and ease of understanding. Always choose clarity over cleverness. Make it easy to understand. Your audience shouldn't have to expend a single additional calorie to decipher what you're saying. If in doubt, get a 12-year-old to read it and explain it back to you.

3. Is it believable? Is your claim, offer, or promise believable? Can a reasonable person from your target market believe you can solve their problem? Even when your message is 100 percent true (which it should be), there may be a credibility or believability gap that you need to overcome. A great way to do this is with proof. For example, instead of saying "the best customer service in the industry," which is vague, hard to believe, and unquantifiable, say "94 percent of first-time buyers become repeat customers." Proof takes an unbelievable-sounding claim and turns it into a fact.

4. Is it interesting or unique? The biggest sin when it comes to messaging is being boring. Can you introduce some novelty factor? It can be in the message, the product, the packaging, or the pricing. I love cross-pollinating ideas from other industries. For example, if your industry doesn't usually offer subscription pricing or a delivery service, that might be something you use to create novelty or differentiation. Rarely does the novelty come from the core deliverable.

5. Is it the good thing without the bad thing? Can I get the result with minimal or no downsides? Think about the most common objections your prospect has. Can you give them the transformation they seek without the perceived risks, downsides, or sacrifices? For example, losing weight without giving up your favorite foods.

6. Is it clear who it's for? When a person from your ideal target market reads or hears your message, their reaction should be, "Hey, that's for me!" This is where foundational elements like target market selection and product-market fit come in. Even when you have these in place, it's important to communicate them clearly and succinctly in short form. A useful tool that can signal who your message is for is a "flag" that precedes the headline. For example, "Dentists in California: Reduce Patient No-Shows and Last-Minute Cancellations by 81%."

The flag "Dentists in California" clearly signals who this message is for before addressing a big problem they're experiencing in their business.

7. Is the next action clear? Give a clear, direct call to action. What's the next physical, visible action they should take? Do you want them to call a phone number, click a link, or enter their email address? Tell them exactly what they should do next.

Pass your short-form message through each of these seven filters to ensure it's magnetic. Once you've drafted your message, ask yourself:

- Is it about them?
- Is it easy to understand?
- Is it believable?
- Is it interesting or unique?
- Is it the good thing without the bad thing?
- Is it clear who it's for?
- Is the next action clear?

Keep editing and refining your message until you hit as many of these as possible.

Chapter 5 Action Items

- Review your content and apply the ten copywriting commandments. Ensure you follow these for all future content.

- Create a content and story bank you can draw from whenever you need to create content.

- Update your short-form marketing messages so they hit as many of the magnetic messaging framework filters as possible.

6

Artificial Intelligence

CHAPTER 6 SUMMARY

Artificial intelligence (AI) is disrupting and will continue to disrupt traditional jobs and industries. Lean marketers use it to create new opportunities and operational efficiencies.

Highlights covered in this chapter include:

- Which businesses and job functions will be harmed by AI and which ones will be enabled by it

- How natural human instincts may be clouding your judgment and what to do about it

- How technology disrupted the music industry and how this relates to your work as a marketer

- How to ensure AI and new technologies become your competitive advantage rather than a threat

- How lean marketers will benefit from AI

- How AI large language models work and how to make the most of their capabilities

- How to avoid using AI the wrong way in writing and content creation

Everything Old Is New Again

Technology is the ultimate disruptive force. It giveth and it taketh away, but mostly it giveth. It has disrupted jobs, businesses, and industries and will continue to do so. If you're on the wrong end of this disruption, you might feel bitter about it and be nostalgic for the "good old days." They aren't coming back, and you're likely looking back through rose-colored glasses.

In the 17th century, there was great concern that the printing press would hinder learning, flood the world with too many books, and foster the dissemination of false, frivolous, or harmful information.

Centuries later, we hear eerily similar concerns about the Internet, social media, and artificial intelligence (AI). There are even concerns that artificial intelligence will literally destroy or take over humanity. I, for one, welcome our silicon overlords. 🤖

With every new wave of technology, we get the same predictable cycle. First comes the hype with over-the-top promises about how the new thing will change everything. Hot new companies emerge. This is followed by panic about it destroying jobs, making us dumb and lazy, and causing society to degenerate. Finally comes mass adoption. It becomes a part of our everyday lives and workflow and makes us more productive.

Artificial Intelligence Versus Natural Stupidity

Humans are hardwired with biases and instincts that make us think and behave in ways that no longer serve us. We have natural stupidity. Understanding this prevents you from being caught up in either the hype or the fear.

In his book *Factfulness*, Hans Rosling lays out ten instincts that distort our perspective. These include the Negativity Instinct— our inclination to notice the bad more than the good; the Fear Instinct—we pay more attention to frightening things; and the Single Perspective Instinct—we prefer simple explanations and clear narratives and often resist complex or multifaceted explanations.

As marketers, we take these instincts into account to make our marketing more effective. As entrepreneurs, we need to beware of them.

If you focus on the news from the usual merchants of doom and gloom, you'd think the world was falling apart. Their business model relies on tapping into our negativity, fear, and single-perspective instincts. The headline "Billions of People Had an Uneventful Day" doesn't generate clicks and attention.

While media, films, and TV shows depict a dystopian future, I don't buy it. We're living in the best time in human history, and the future is only getting brighter. King Solomon, in all his glory, didn't have a life as good as the average person does today (although, to be fair, it sounds like he did have a lot of fun).

That's not to say that all problems are solved. There are still many challenges to address. However, if the progress over the last few hundred years is any indication, technology and now AI will help solve many of them.

It's inevitable that AI will become superintelligent, meaning that it will surpass the intelligence of the brightest and most gifted human minds. Whether it takes over and starts farming humans for energy is still an open question. If that does happen, you'll have much bigger problems than marketing. My hope is that this fate will be limited to people who have "Futurist" in their LinkedIn bio.

There's a solid track record of science fiction turning into science fact. The series *Star Trek: The Next Generation* is a rite of passage for geeks. One of the main characters in it is a humanoid robot named Data. He can do anything that a human can do but better. He's smarter, stronger, and faster. Throughout the series, he grapples with understanding and emulating human emotion and behavior. Despite his superior abilities, he spends most of his time in service to humanity. I suspect this will be the case with superintelligent AI. It'll try in vain to figure out why we do what we do and be of service to us in the process.

Software Is Eating the World

Many of the tools and innovations that will either disrupt you or enable you will be software. Venture capitalist Marc Andreessen famously said that software is eating the world. Most of the time, when I leave my house, the only item I take is my smartphone. Software on it has "eaten" so many of the physical items I used to need, like a music player, camera, GPS navigation unit, laptop, garage door opener, wallet, and credit cards.

Regardless of your industry, you must assume that a software breakthrough is coming. You can either eat or be eaten.

Process-driven jobs and businesses will be gone. This is a good thing. That's the boring, repetitive, and dangerous stuff. People often think of so-called blue-collar workers being disrupted: drivers, packagers, assembly line workers. These will be heavily impacted, but so will process-driven white-collar work like law, accounting, medicine, and, of course, marketing.

Any sufficiently repeatable or predictable functions will eventually get automated, slowly at first and then all at once. Creative work and creative components of work will be all that is left. An AI tool might do the heavy lifting of drafting a long and complex legal contract, but you'll still need the creative skills of a lawyer or banker to structure and negotiate a deal.

You don't have to be a technology geek to be on the right side of the software food chain. However, you must be open to using technology as a force multiplier in your business. AI won't take your job or disrupt your business, but someone using AI will.

Disruption, Not Destruction

A common fear with almost every major technological breakthrough is destruction. This fear is justified, but it's only part of the story. Focusing only on loss prevents you from seeing huge opportunities.

I've seen this movie many times before and know how it ends. AI will destroy some jobs, businesses, and industries but create many new ones. Huge amounts of wealth will be created. In a paper about emerging jobs, researcher David Autor noted that 60 percent of all employment in 2018 was from jobs that didn't exist in 1940. Indeed, Who ever imagined YouTuber, gamer, or podcaster could be jobs? AI will only accelerate this trend.

You can be the old man on the lawn shaking his fist and shouting, "You kids don't understand the meaning of hard work!" or you can embrace the new jobs, businesses, and industries it will create, enable, and scale.

In 1930, the union of American singers spent the equivalent of $10 million on a campaign to prevent people from listening to recorded music and watching movies with sound.

A "PROFIT" Without Honor

PART 7—PAGE 2

Artists Fight Against Use of "Canned" Music

Thousands Lose Jobs; Talkies to Blame.

The advent of recorded sound in films drastically reduced the employment of local musicians. In 1927, there were around 24,000 musicians employed in theaters across the United States and Canada. With the arrival of the first talking film, *The Jazz Singer*, many of these jobs disappeared. By 1930, 30 percent of these musicians had lost their jobs. In some markets, musician unemployment reached 50–75 percent.

However, new technology doesn't just destroy. It's a creative force that spawns new and bigger opportunities.

Records, radio, and talking films made creative work cheaper and more accessible to a much larger audience. Three hundred musicians in Hollywood could now supply all the music offered in thousands of theaters.

At the time, it seemed unlikely that "canned music" would replace "real" music. As we now know, it didn't. It supplemented, scaled, and supported it. Mediocre musicians have indeed suffered losses, but the live music industry is bigger than ever. Many musicians make most of their income from concerts, live events, and merchandise. This is driven by the audiences they've built up through their recorded music.

The Lean Marketer's Toolkit

As AI has become more powerful, much of the volume-based manual work marketers have had to do is disappearing. Lean marketing principles have become critical as marketers shift their focus to activities that create value for their target market. To use lean terminology, your work as a marketer is now primarily in the "value stream."

Like recorded music disrupted musicians a century ago, many routine, labor-intensive, and operational marketing tasks are being streamlined, scaled, and automated with AI.

Specialized AI tools have made editing and creating images, videos, and audio content easier, cheaper, and faster. More general-purpose AI tools like large language models are impressive and can generate human-like text based on your input. They also allow you to do various tasks like making sense of data, writing code, and answering complex queries.

As expressed in the previous chapter, words are the building blocks of everything you do in marketing. Therefore, it's worth paying attention to the impact these large language models are having on writing.

If your writing is mediocre, boring, and volume-based, it's already game over for you. You'll go the way of the local musicians who lost their jobs. These large language models can pump out unlimited amounts of this kind of content.

However, I doubt these models will ever produce great writing. This is inherent in their design. They don't understand words like humans do. They don't have beliefs, opinions, or consciousness. AI large language models learn by studying patterns in massive amounts of text data.

The main job of the model is prediction. Given a sequence of words, it tries to predict the next word, kind of like a very advanced autocorrect. For example, if you give it "The sky is…," it might predict and generate "blue" as the next word because it has learned that "blue" often follows "The sky is."

By their very design, such models will predict the most common patterns. This results in a lot of clichés and generic writing. If the model's output was too unpredictable, it would generate text that wouldn't make sense.

To manage this, these models use a randomness setting called "temperature" during the generation process. If the temperature is set lower, the model chooses the most probable next word. This leads to more predictable and coherent sentences, but these tend to be somewhat generic or clichéd. If the temperature is set higher, the model chooses less probable words. This results in more diverse and creative outputs, but these can sometimes be nonsensical or unrelated to the context.

Large language models particularly excel at tasks with definitive "right" answers that heavily depend on structures, patterns, or rules, such as in programming or legal documentation. This is because these structures are often repeated in the training data, and the model can learn those patterns. However, creativity involves a degree of originality and novelty that can be challenging for a model that learns by finding patterns in existing data.

You can't rely on large language models to do the writing for you if you're going to produce great writing and, therefore, great marketing. There's simply no substitute for your unique stories, experiences, and perspectives. While they're mediocre writers, they make excellent writing assistants.

Large language models have become part of my everyday toolkit, just like search engines and remote collaboration tools did in the past. With tasks like writing, I use them in powerful ways to improve and augment my abilities. I use them for research, summarization, copy editing, refining my writing, and brainstorming. I find new ways to use them every day.

Go to the Lean Marketing Hub to look over my shoulder and see how I use AI tools and large language models in my marketing and writing. Visit LeanMarketing.com/hub

Many AI tools have natural language interfaces, which means that people who can write with clarity of thought are the most skilled at using them. Writers are essentially the new software engineers.

AI is truly the Iron Man suit for marketers, allowing you to do more with less and helping you build a truly lean marketing infrastructure. I think of it as enabling us to be the conductor of the orchestra rather than having to play each individual instrument.

Chapter 6 Action Items

- Identify manual, process-driven tasks in your business and marketing systems. Then, research tools and technologies that can do the heavy lifting for you.

- Where does friction exist in your customer journey? Embed tools and technologies that will help reduce friction and improve the customer experience.

- Integrate AI tools into your content creation workflows to reduce time, cost, and effort while increasing output and quality.

FORCE MULTIPLIER 2

ASSETS

Why the Rich Get Richer

I grew up in a family of very modest means. My parents were first-generation immigrants, and like many others, they moved a long way to make a better life for their children. I thank them every day for the sacrifices they made. Basic government assistance combined with hard work ensured we always had a roof over our heads and enough to eat.

In my family, references to wealthy people were almost always accompanied by the words "greedy" or "dishonest." My only understanding of wealth came from cartoons of Scrooge McDuck diving into his vault full of gold coins and money.

It was only when I started my first business that I got exposed to successful entrepreneurs and business owners. Many had amassed fortunes but didn't fit what I had been taught wealthy people were like. The vast majority of them were generous, easygoing, and helpful.

Not long after that, I recall buying my first personal development book, *Rich Dad Poor Dad*, by Robert Kiyosaki. I distinctly remember trying to read it in secret because I felt embarrassed that my family might think I was trying to become a greedy, dishonest, rich person.

While *Rich Dad Poor Dad* has many flaws, it was my introduction to financial literacy and helped me understand basic concepts like assets and liabilities. The book's definition of an asset is beautiful in its simplicity—an asset is something that puts money in your pocket whether you work or not.

Over time, my views on money and wealth have changed dramatically. Obviously, I no longer view the wealthy with suspicion.

Along the way, I've also learned a lot of lessons about wealth and money. Perhaps the most important one is that **the wealthy derive their income predominantly from assets rather than labor.** Assets are what separate the have-nots from the have-yachts.

If you own real estate, you can earn rental income. If you own stocks, you can earn dividends.

If you don't own assets, your only option is to earn with your labor. There's nothing wrong with that, but it's not scalable, it's not salable, and your earnings stop when you stop. By contrast, assets generate income passively. When paired with labor to operate or upgrade them, assets become powerful force multipliers, significantly amplifying these labor inputs.

Build Marketing Assets

Marketing assets work in a very similar way. They can help you generate leads, prospects, and customers and turn these into revenue and profit for your business. They're your key to doing less marketing and getting bigger and better results.

LEAN MARKETING PRINCIPLE 5:
Use assets to increase your yield on marketing activities

If your marketing assets are nonexistent or weak, you'll have to compensate with time, money, and labor. You'll have to resort to labor-intensive "hunting" activities like cold calling, constant prospecting, and networking. If you've got solid marketing assets, it's a lot more like farming. You plant, you water, and you harvest.

Both hunting and farming are important contributors to a well-rounded marketing system. However, relying solely on hunting is marketing the hard way. And when you stop, the lead flow stops.

If generating new business is an uphill battle for you, that's a symptom that you don't have marketing assets working for you. If your customer acquisition cost is too high, that's another symptom.

If you want to build an oil well, it's hard work doing the research, getting the permits, designing it, and building it. But once it's built, you just keep it operating, pumping the oil out of the ground and profiting.

Assets are a huge force multiplier when it comes to marketing. That's why I encourage clients to spend significant time and effort creating new marketing assets or upgrading existing ones. The exciting thing is that once built, they can continuously generate lead flow and profit with minimal labor inputs.

Marketing is often thought of as an expense, but if you build marketing assets, you'll start seeing it more like a capital investment. To generate higher yields, you invest in improving the asset. For example, if you wanted to double the production capacity of your oil well, would you need to work twice as hard? Would you need to be twice as smart? Would you need to be twice as lucky? Of course not. You'd invest capital to make the required improvements. You'd work with your engineers to make changes to the system: drill deeper, adjust the crank position, or upgrade the pumps. You'd then reap the benefits of your capital investment.

The same is true of your marketing assets. They are upgradable. As you improve them over time, they'll generate higher and higher yields. You'll eliminate waste, increase efficiency, and create more value for your target market. As a result, you'll pump out more leads, more prospects, and, ultimately, more customers from your marketing system.

7

Your Brand (Start with Buy)

CHAPTER 7 SUMMARY

Few things cause as much confusion and waste as "branding." Yet building a strong brand is one of the most powerful and profitable things you can do in your business.

Highlights covered in this chapter include:

- Why popular business advice is leading you astray and what really leads to business success

- What a brand truly is, without the fluff and jargon

- The purpose of your brand and where strong brands come from

- What customers actually care about when it comes to your brand

- How to measure the strength of your brand

- How to charge a premium for your products and services

- Why selling is the best way to build a brand

The Passion Delusion

What I'm about to say will either anger you or set you free.

A large part of what I do every day is take entrepreneurs from stuck to unstuck. Sometimes, being stuck is self-inflicted, but most of the time, it's the result of bad advice from consultants, celebrities, and crazies.

Everybody says, "Follow your passion." Figure out your vision, your mission, and your core values. The first few chapters of practically every business and self-help book is stuff like this. Rather than being helpful, this nonsense has kept many people stuck.

One book I recently read says, "It has to be something bigger than yourself or making money." Why? Why can't I just bring value to the marketplace and capture a fraction of it? Is having some fun, helping some people, and making a heap of money in the process OK? Could we still succeed without a grand vision, lofty mission, and passion dripping from the sky? I think so.

I'm exaggerating a little here, but only a little. I'm passionate about what I do. I look forward to Mondays. I love my clients. I get a buzz when I get messages from raving fans. I love helping entrepreneurs build extraordinary businesses and live life on their own terms. It feels great to turn on the light for someone who didn't have a light.

All this makes me passionate about what I do, but chances are I'd be a lot less passionate if I was struggling financially. In fact, I'd be pretty bummed out. I'd probably hate Mondays. I probably wouldn't be as excited about working with my clients. Financial success fuels passion far more often than the reverse.

Yeah, yeah, I know the best things in life are free. I hear you. I also enjoy pretty sunsets, wagging dog tails, and the warmth of a crackling fire. But money buys some cool stuff, too. It also enhances the free stuff *a lot*.

The view of the sunset over the bay from my beach house feels sweeter than when I lived in a rented hovel in a crowded suburb, surrounded by neighbors screaming at each other.

My dog's tail wags better with world-class veterinary care. I compare this to when, as a kid, my dog was hit by a car, and my mom rehabilitated him herself because paying a vet was an extravagance we didn't even imagine was an option.

So what comes first, passion or success? Look, there's no denying some people are just born with something they feel a great passion for. They know they've been put on this earth to do what they do. But they're a minority. For the rest of us, it will be a journey of trying many things, looking for opportunities, and being curious. I'm still trying to figure out what I want to be when I "grow up." Parts of your journey will be dead ends, while others will lead you to the promised land.

Take someone who makes millions of dollars manufacturing screws. Did they wake up one day and say, "Wow, I'm so passionate about screws. I'm going to put everything on the line to make screws that change the world." Probably not. Where are all the passionate industrial cleaners, office supply wholesalers, and pest controllers?

More likely, they saw an opportunity in the marketplace, had a skill or capital, and put it to good use, building a profitable business. And guess what? Now they're passionate about it. Correlation, not causation.

Most of the time, passion follows success rather than being a prerequisite for it. Put another way, passion, like profit, is a result. You don't find your passion. It finds *you*. As you try new things, follow your curiosity, and discover your aptitude, you create a larger surface area for passion to develop.

Instead of "do what you love," a more effective mantra for the entrepreneur is "love what you do." Do what you love is for amateurs. Love what you do is for professionals. Prolific British author William Somerset Maugham was once asked if he wrote by inspiration or habit. He replied, "I write only when inspiration strikes. Fortunately, it strikes every morning at nine o'clock sharp." That's how professionals do it.

What about your favorite business celebrities like Richard Branson or Steve Jobs, who've said the secret to success is following your passion? If Steve Jobs had founded a kitchenware manufacturer instead of a computer hardware company, I bet he would have been passionate about that, and we'd have the world's most beautiful kitchen utensils. We'd probably be upgrading our iFryingPan to the newest model each year.

I also find it an amazing coincidence that Richard Branson is passionate about anything and everything that makes a profit, from airlines to mobile phones. Most billionaires telling you to follow your passion made their wealth from boring stuff like real estate, finance, and ordinary products.

I'm not against passion. If you have it, more power to you. Use it as fuel. If you're unsure about your passion, don't worry—you're in good company. Sometimes, your fuel burns dirty, and your drivers are fear, desperation, or revenge. These can be just as effective or even more so. Use the fuel you've got, not the fuel you wish you had. Get where you want to go and work the rest out with your therapist once you're there.

Some passions are impossible to monetize. I'm passionate about walking and hiking through beautiful forest areas, but no one wants to pay me to do that. (Some will say that's my cue to start a hiking boot company.)

This leads to the next issue related to "following your passion." About 99 percent of the stuff you need to do to build a business around your passion will have nothing to do with the actual thing you're passionate about. If I were to start a hiking boot company, I'd need to spend most of my time on the usual company-building stuff like design, manufacturing, sales, and marketing—not hiking.

The better advice is to follow your efforts, your curiosity, and your opportunities. When you put time into something, you get better at it. When you get better at it, you have a chance to be great at it. Rarely does anyone quit something they're great at. Once you get great at it, it's amazing how passionate you'll become about it.

Ignore What Simon Says

The business equivalent of "follow your passion" is Simon Sinek's one-liner "Start with Why," which became a famous TED Talk and then book. Now, it's a management consulting wet dream. It's the subject of endless meetings and corporate retreats. The best part is, at the end of all those billable hours, you end up with something that can't really be quantified. After all, there's no wrong "why," is there?

Throughout this TED Talk, Simon emphatically repeats, "People don't buy what you do. They buy why you do it." This is very seductive because your organization can change its "why" after a one-day offsite. Changing what you sell and whom you sell to is a lot harder.

Every example I've ever heard of "starting with why" looked to me much more like revisionist history than deliberate strategy. Descriptive rather than prescriptive. It has become a running joke that every tech startup in Silicon Valley has the purported mission "to make the world a better place."

Simon Sinek made finding your "why" trendy, but I think it did more harm than good. Wasting resources on mental masturbation takes your eyes off the prize. Your early success is often a result of desperation-induced focus. As your business grows and desperation is no longer in the driver's seat, it's critical to maintain your focus. I've seen too many good businesses plateau once they reach a comfortable level of success because they got distracted with virtue signaling, politics, or bureaucracy.

I'm not against Simon. I like him. He's a super-smart guy and an incredible speaker. I'm also not against having a higher purpose for what you do in your business. If you have some incredible "why" that drives you and your team, then by all means, use it. But know that only your mother and best friend buy your stuff because of "why you do it." The rest of us buy *what* you do.

But here's what irritates me most. Someone with an entrepreneurial dream:

- Creates jobs
- Creates wealth
- Helps drive the economy forward
- Creates a good life for themselves and their family
- Pays taxes
- Creates a lot of value and takes only a fraction of it
- Donates to charity
- Creates a return for investors
- Takes care of customers
- Inspires and cares for employees

Then some bozo consultant who's never actually run a business comes along and tells them all of this isn't good enough—they need to break their heads coming up with a "why" to shoehorn into their "brand purpose." One that'll make them look noble. What could possibly be more noble than the things on that list? Do you really need a bigger "why" than all that stuff?

It feels almost taboo to dismiss someone's "why." After all, how can you argue with a noble purpose? If I'm not already, let me be clear: the most noble purpose of your business is to make a profit.

If you're a social enterprise or charity, then sure, starting with "why" could make sense. If you're a for-profit business, start with buy, not why.

What Is a Brand?

Nothing generates as much waste in marketing as so-called brand building.

This starts predictably with a workshop on the business' core values. You'll come up with the usual clichés like honesty, hard work, quality, accountability, communication, and so on. Not that any of these are bad. They're just eye-rollingly obvious and are baseline expectations. Yet, listing them is treated like some kind of amazing discovery.

As time goes on, it gets weirder, and you end up with weasel words like "synergy," "core competency," "paradigm shift," and worse.

I used to assume the reason I didn't understand what the heck these people were talking about was because they were smart and I was dumb.

That changed when I came across the work of the Nobel Prize–winning physicist Richard Feynman. Feynman's genius was his ability to convey complex ideas in simple and elegant ways. The Feynman Rule is: if someone uses a lot of complexity and jargon to explain something to you, they probably don't understand it.

So here's my Feynman-inspired definition of a brand: **A brand is the personality of a business.**

Just as many different elements make up an individual's personality, many elements make up a brand. Your name, how you dress, and how you communicate make up some of your personality, but it's much more than just that.

Most people who claim to be building a brand obsess about colors, fonts, and logos. If a brand is the personality of a business, then these visual design aspects are analogous to how someone dresses. These elements are not inconsequential but certainly not their whole personality or the main reason you'd build a close relationship with them.

Maya Angelou famously said, "People will forget what you said, people will forget what you did, but people will never forget how you made them feel."

How someone makes you feel is core to your relationship with them. Many brand marketers recognize this and try to evoke these feelings through design, ads, and imagery. This is OK, but it's difficult, expensive, and often has limited cut-through. It's like trying to create and maintain a love connection in a long-distance relationship.

You might look at great brands like Nike, Apple, and Coca-Cola and conclude that their success comes from flashy ads, big billboards, and expensive sponsorships. But all this is a *result* of their sales success, not the cause of it.

LEAN MARKETING PRINCIPLE 6:
Selling is the best way to build a brand

Nike started with its founder, Phil Knight, selling running shoes from the trunk of his car at track meets and local sporting events.

Coca-Cola started with Dr. John S. Pemberton selling it as a syrup at soda fountains in pharmacies.

Apple started with Steve Jobs and Steve Wozniak selling single-board computers to hobbyists and enthusiasts in computer clubs and electronics stores.

What better way is there for someone to experience the personality of your business than actually working with you? Show, don't tell. That's why we start with buy.

Your Brand Purpose

I love accountants. While I don't fully understand their world, as a nerd, I feel like they're kindred spirits. I ask them a question, and I get a straight answer. Usually, they give me my favorite type of straight answer—a number.

Under both GAAP and IFRS, the two most widely accepted accounting standards, the value of a brand you've created can't be recognized on your balance sheet. This is because a brand is an "intangible asset," which is accounting-speak for "it's all in your head." As we'd expect from our bean-counter buddies, this is quite accurate. A brand exists in the mind of your target market.

The situation differs a bit if a brand is bought or sold. When money has been exchanged for a brand, accountants get excited and put a line item on your balance sheet called "goodwill."

Goodwill represents the amount paid above the value of easily quantifiable assets. For example, say you acquired a company for $10 million. If it had $3 million in inventory and $5 million in plant and equipment at the time of purchase, that means you paid $2 million for "goodwill." A good chunk of that goodwill is the value of the brand.

"Goodwill" is a great word when thinking about branding. It represents the extra value created over and above the tangible.

So, when you hear someone talking about "brand purpose," politely excuse yourself. The rest of what they're about to tell you is usually utter nonsense.

Your brand has only one purpose: to enable you to charge a premium above the intrinsic value of what you do. As our accountant friends would put it, it's goodwill—goodwill that your customers are willing to pay for. If the customer doesn't pay a premium, you don't have a brand.

Where Do Brands Come From?

The question "Where do brands come from?" is the business equivalent of a child asking, "Where do babies come from?" What follows is usually awkward silence followed by a bunch of euphemisms. Let's not do that. You've gotten this far in the book so you must be OK with a bit of straight talk.

When a customer and a company love each other very much, a brand gets created. A brand is wonderful because it enables the company to charge more for what they do than its commodity value. A brand makes customers, employees, and shareholders happy, and they all live happily ever after.

I'm not being cute. This is really it.

Think about a friend or family member you love dearly. Would you go to more expense and effort to help them than you would a stranger? Kindness to strangers is important, but your beloved friend or family member would likely get far more of your time, resources, and attention because they've built up a large goodwill "account" with you.

Similarly, you build a strong brand by making regular deposits of goodwill with your target market. All other things being equal, people prefer to buy from someone they know, like, and trust.

Typical marketers get overdrawn through constant hype, scams, and pressure, which creates negative brand value. The only way to compensate for this is to discount prices.

By contrast, lean marketers create goodwill and brand equity. They do this by delivering a world-class customer experience, building strong intellectual property, and ensuring their marketing is helpful, entertaining, and valuable.

I'll dive deep into specific ways to achieve these things in the following chapters.

Chapter 7 Action Items

- What's the personality of your business from a customer's perspective? Review your entire customer journey and perhaps even go undercover and purchase from your own business to experience what your customers are experiencing.

- Review all your marketing material for congruence and consistency with how you want customers to feel.

- Consider ways your business can generate more goodwill with prospects and customers.

8

Your Flagship Asset

CHAPTER 8 SUMMARY

Building trust, goodwill, and brand equity is a huge marketing challenge. A flagship marketing asset can help you do this while creating a lot of value for your audience.

Highlights covered in this chapter include:

- How to create a marketing asset that will help you build trust, generate leads, support your sales efforts, and stimulate referrals

- Examples of successful flagship assets

- A counterintuitive way of generating revenue by giving away a lot of value

- How to powerfully demonstrate to your ideal prospect that you can actually help them

- How to create a "tripwire" that turns invisible prospects into visible ones at the exact right time in the buying cycle

- Why it's important to center your flagship asset on a "big idea"

- Common mistakes made with flagship marketing assets and how to avoid them

Results in Advance

A lot of marketing is focused on making promises about how great life will be for your prospect after they purchase your product or service. This is fine, but the problem is everyone is out there making the same claims, so it's hard to stand out from the crowd. Worse, your prospects have been burned by broken promises many times and don't believe you. Your flagship asset helps you overcome this by showing rather than telling.

Instead of promising to be helpful once they become a customer, your flagship asset actually helps your target market get a result in advance of them buying from you. It creates a lot of value for them, and if you do it well, you'll be famous for that thing within your target market.

A flagship asset can be used in numerous ways, including supporting your sales process, stimulating referrals, and, of course, generating leads. It's a powerful way to create trust, goodwill, and brand equity and convert these into revenue.

Most commonly, your flagship asset is a piece of content, but not always. I'll share some examples in a moment. While a flagship asset can be used to attract leads, it differs from what's commonly referred to as a "lead magnet."

A lead magnet is some valuable content or incentive you give in exchange for a prospect's contact information or an action you want them to take. Lead magnets tend to be much more specific. If you're running ten different ad campaigns, you might have ten different lead magnets because you want them to be highly relevant to the ad copy.

Your flagship asset is more expansive. When used for lead generation, you might think of it as your primary broad-spectrum lead magnet.

Typically, your flagship asset is free, but it doesn't have to be. It can be a low-cost, entry-level glimpse into your world and what you do. Beyond just lead generation, the goal of a flagship asset is to:

- demonstrate that you can help your ideal prospect by actually helping them.

- highlight, exaggerate, and crystallize your uniqueness.

- turn invisible prospects into visible ones.

- build trust, goodwill, and brand equity regardless of whether they buy from you or not.

A flagship asset is a powerful stepping stone between the pain your prospect is currently experiencing and the pain relief that you offer.

Your flagship asset is centered on a "big idea." By big, I don't necessarily mean grandiose. I mean something that makes your ideal target market pay attention and think, "I want that." This will differ depending on your business, but typically, it's a piece of content, an experience, or a tool.

Flagship Content

In 1900, the Michelin brothers, André and Édouard, founders of the Michelin tire company, launched the Michelin Guide, which awards stars to fine-dining establishments. A 1-star award is "a very good restaurant in its category," 2 stars is "excellent cooking, worth a detour," and 3 stars is "exceptional cuisine, worth a special journey."

If you're a tire company in the 1900s, tapping into a rapidly increasing market of drivers and getting your customers to drive more is good for business. If you're the owner of this new form of transport that can take you places faster and farther than ever before, having a guide with great places to go is very helpful. It's a win-win. This is a classic example of a flagship piece of content.

Naming and claiming your unique process, framework, or methodology is a solid starting point for creating a flagship piece of content. Even if what you do isn't unique, it gives your prospect something to differentiate you by in a sea of sameness.

For service-based businesses, a flagship piece of content is often the do-it-yourself (DIY) version of what you do or a tool that helps your target market move towards a solution to their problem.

A common objection to giving away your know-how is, "If I give away my secrets, why would anyone buy my services?" I've never seen a single instance where giving away knowledge, ideas, or expertise in a DIY or tool form truly cannibalized service revenue. The polar opposite is usually true.

The more airplay a song gets, the more popular it becomes. As it increases in popularity, it creates sales and streaming revenue, and more people want to see the performer live in concert. Your business will also experience an uplift in interest and revenue when you share your best stuff generously. Conventional wisdom tells you to save the best for last. But conventional wisdom leads to conventional outcomes. Instead, save the best for first and lead with massive value.

A common frustration of service-based businesses is that prospects underappreciate the skill and expertise needed to deliver those services. Sometimes, you're so good that you make what you do look easy. People only pay for value they recognize. Giving away a DIY version is a great way to demonstrate what's really involved in getting the result your prospect wants. It also creates goodwill, builds trust, and fuels their imagination about the enormous value they'd get if they became a paying customer.

Someone who's a genuine prospect in your target market will almost always prefer to pay you to do it for them or with them. A concertgoer is paying for a very different experience when they attend a concert than when they listen to those same songs at home for free. Similarly, struggling through a DIY process in an area outside your expertise is a very different experience from working with an expert who navigates you safely through to your desired result.

If you want to position yourself as a thought leader, a nonfiction book is the gold standard flagship piece of content. I think of it as the nuclear weapon of business cards. Writing a book is hard, but it can open a lot of doors. Even if someone doesn't read your entire book or even any of it, it's a powerful positioning tool. You'll be invited to speak and be interviewed, opening up opportunities you wouldn't otherwise have had. Another thing I like about books is that people tend to keep them for years because throwing them out feels like a sin. We've been conditioned from an early age to respect books and, by extension, authors.

A how-to guide can work well if you sell a tool of some kind. For example, I recently saw a company that sells survey software to marketers offer "The Marketer's Guide to Surveying Users." Another software company that sells helpdesk software gave away a comprehensive guide on best practices for customer support.

Awards or leaderboards are another style of flagship content. The Michelin Guide is an example of this. Other examples include the Forbes 30 Under 30, the Billboard Hot 100, and the Inc. 5000.

White papers, case studies, and research reports with commentary can be powerful in business-to-business markets. For example, Akamai Technologies, a content delivery network and cybersecurity company behind some of the world's biggest websites, regularly releases *State of the Internet* reports. These are useful for their prospects and customers but also generate a lot of industry press. If you've ever seen an article that ranks the Internet speed of various countries, Akamai's report is often the source.

Structured data reports can work well for industries where pricing or other data is opaque, hard to find, or hard to interpret. For example, some realtors offer a report detailing house sale prices in their area for the last 90 days. This is useful to prospective buyers who want to know what properties are within their budget. It's also useful to someone considering selling and wanting to know what their property might be worth. The Rapaport Price List, often referred to simply as the Rap List, is well known in the diamond industry. It provides a benchmark for diamond pricing and has helped establish a standard in the global market.

Depending on what you do, different types of flagship content might be more or less appropriate for your audience. Ideally, you'll have an element that needs to be updated periodically or have some other reason to keep your audience connected and paying attention to you.

Sometimes, the lines between flagship content and ongoing content marketing processes are blurred. For example, a podcast or YouTube channel might be an important part of your content marketing efforts. It may bring you fame within your target market, provide a lot of value to your audience, and achieve a lot of what a flagship piece of content does. (I discuss content marketing in more detail in Chapter 13.)

Flagship Experiences

A flagship experience can give prospects a taster, nurture demand, and share your personality or uniqueness in an exaggerated way. For example, Red Bull runs or sponsors various extreme sports that entertain, inspire, and clearly demonstrate extremeness and energy. Flagship experiences can also provide fuel for your content marketing efforts.

A signature keynote blends a flagship piece of content and a flagship experience. For example, Arnold Schwarzenegger, David Goggins, Brené Brown, and Tony Robbins have delivered similar messages and keynotes for decades. Just like a hit song, once you have a formula that connects, you can deliver it repeatedly and distribute it in various modalities and formats.

The Macy's Thanksgiving Day Parade, TechCrunch Disrupt, and Victoria's Secret Fashion Show are all examples of flagship experiences used to create goodwill, nurture demand, and showcase their values and personality.

I'll leave you with a word of caution regarding flagship experiences. For many businesses, this should be considered an advanced strategy. There's a risk it will turn into an expensive "brand building" exercise with little connection to any kind of return on investment.

As covered in the previous chapter, real brand building comes from sales. Have your core fundamentals in place before trying to outdo the likes of Red Bull.

A better use of resources early on for most smaller businesses can be offering a taster, trial, or sample of what you do. We've all walked through a mall where delicious free samples have caused us to buy when we otherwise probably wouldn't have. This is often a much more direct path to getting a return while also being experiential.

Some car manufacturers and dealerships have "drive days" where current and prospective customers experience different models within the make.

As with all your marketing activities, test and measure. Then, double down on the winners and cut the losers.

Flagship Tools

Richard Buckminster Fuller said, "If you want to teach people a new way of thinking, don't bother trying to teach them. Instead, give them a tool, the use of which will lead to new ways of thinking." Flagship tools are powerful in guiding your prospect's thinking.

They can use them to assess where they currently stand and start on the path to a better situation. An example is the Love Language Quiz, which helps you determine which of the five love languages is your primary one and what this might mean for your love life.

Scorecards are also great flagship tools because whenever you give someone a score, their natural inclination will be to improve it—which is often where your product or service comes in. I love quizzes and scorecards as flagship tools because collecting data about your prospect is a feature rather than a bug.

Google Analytics is a tool that Google offers for free to website owners. It's great for Google in two ways. Firstly, it gives them an enormous amount of data and insights into billions of websites. Secondly, someone measuring their website traffic is the perfect target to sell paid digital ads to, as they likely want to increase their visitor numbers. It's a virtuous cycle of revealing a problem and then providing the solution to solve it.

For years, HubSpot has offered a free Website Grader tool that analyzes your site and then offers helpful suggestions on improving it. People keen on improving their inbound marketing performance are an ideal target market for HubSpot's CRM platform and software tools. Dharmesh Shah, the co-founder of HubSpot, has often highlighted how the Website Grader was one of their earliest and most effective lead-generation tools.

Various graphic design and image editing apps offer free stand-alone tools like color palette generators. Many website builder platforms offer a free logo creator. Again, people interested in creating a color palette or logo are natural prospects for graphic design and website builder software.

These flagship tools are genuinely helpful in a stand-alone capacity while also creating a natural way to move potential prospects to the next step in the buying cycle. While most users of the free tools may never become paying customers, many will.

A large part of the magic behind *The 1-Page Marketing Plan* is the canvas. It's a tool that allows you to create an easy-to-understand, easy-to-share, and easy-to-update marketing plan in as little as 20 minutes. The book wouldn't have been anywhere near as successful or impactful had I left out the canvas, even if it had the same information. Tools help guide our ways of thinking.

Making Invisible Prospects Visible

Some prospects are visible, meaning we can easily get a list of them. For example, you could get a list of all the personal injury lawyers in the state of Texas. However, many other types of prospects are invisible, so we need them to identify themselves. Your flagship asset acts like a tripwire, revealing invisible prospects and turning them into visible ones.

For example, out of the billions of people on the Internet, how would we find people with diabetes who might be in the market for a continuous glucose monitoring device? They're an invisible prospect. But someone downloading a flagship asset titled "The Diabetic's Guide to Continuous Glucose Monitoring" is making themselves visible. They're highly likely to be a diabetic who is interested in continuous glucose monitoring. You'd almost have to question someone's sanity if they downloaded "The Diabetic's Guide to Continuous Glucose Monitoring" and weren't a diabetic interested in continuous glucose monitoring.

This is a highly efficient way of revealing high-probability invisible prospects. Importantly, it's also an early warning mechanism revealing them at the perfect time in the buying cycle.

Timing is a critical factor for one-off or infrequent purchases. Someone requesting a guide on unique destination wedding ideas is highly likely to be in the planning phase of a wedding.

The Pull of Your Big Idea

Most of the examples of flagship assets I've given are centered on a big idea that entices a specific market segment and gets them thinking, "I want that." This could be finding out how much their house is worth, figuring out their love language, racing around a track in a car model they like, or watching beautiful women parade around in lingerie.

A mistake people make with flagship assets (and lead magnets in general) is using them to brag about themselves or making them just a useless teaser. Your flagship content should be valuable, feel neutral, and build goodwill. Your audience concluding that you're awesome is so much more powerful than you saying so.

Another common mistake is forcing prospects to give up lots of information or forcing them to get in touch with your sales team before giving them your flagship asset. It's important to capture their details in your CRM system, but at the beginning, when trust is low, capture the minimal viable data possible. While you want your flagship asset to generate revenue, from a mindset standpoint, treat it like a public service.

Many times, I've been interested in someone's flagship content or tool (even if they didn't call it that), and then when I went to request it, they asked me for a voluminous amount of contact information up front. In these cases, I usually abandon the form unless I'm absolutely certain I want to speak to one of their sales reps. No one wants to be bombarded by salespeople when they're not ready to buy.

Often, when we're excited about what we do, we think about our ideal target market at point A and then jump directly to them using our product or service at point B. However, it would be more accurate to think of this as point A and point Z. There are many steps for your prospect between problem awareness and buying, especially for purchases with a high consideration threshold. Your job is to patiently move them to points B, C, and so on until you ultimately reach point Z.

To create a powerful flagship asset, it's essential to think upstream. After your prospect becomes problem aware, what will help them along the way to solving their problem? A good flagship asset raises your prospect's level of problem awareness, and, importantly, in the process, it actually helps them.

For example, if you recruit salespeople in the healthcare industry, the end goal might be to get prospects to sign a recruitment agreement with you. However, offering current compensation data for salespeople in their industry would be genuinely helpful to them. Someone requesting this content also reveals themselves as a high-probability prospect.

Use your flagship asset as a pulling force towards you rather than something you withhold until you're sure there'll be an equal exchange of value. Be generous with it. Many people interested in what you do may not be ready to buy immediately due to a timing, budget, or trust issue. There'll also be many others who will never buy from you at all but will still consume or use your flagship asset. This is still valuable.

"Abundance" is one of those words thrown around by life coaches, woo-woo people, and weirdos, but it's really at the heart of value-based marketing. Being generous with your flagship asset creates a positive energy around what you do that will come back to you in many forms. As mentioned earlier, you're selling human-to-human, and humans are connectors. You don't know whose hands your flagship asset will eventually end up in or how it will affect them.

Zig Ziglar said, "You can have everything in life you want, if you will just help other people get what they want." Your flagship asset is a great vehicle for doing exactly this.

Chapter 8 Action Items

- Start with a "big idea." What will be genuinely helpful to your target market and make them think, "I want that"?

- Consider whether a flagship experience, tool, or piece of content would be the best way to bring this big idea to life and create a "beta" version of it.

- Share your flagship asset with your audience and pay close attention to their feedback.

9

Your Website

CHAPTER 9 SUMMARY

Most websites are simply online brochures that fail to convert visitors into leads or customers. If structured well, your website can become a powerful revenue-generating asset.

Highlights covered in this chapter include:

- How to stop your website from becoming a "leaky bucket" that isn't performing

- The importance of giving your website a clear "job" and key performance indicators (KPIS)

- How to use content upgrades as a powerful tool for capturing website visitors

- How to use landing pages to ensure your paid ads convert well

- The three-step structure for the "hero section" of your home page that compels visitors to take action

- How to choose your website's domain name

- The most important design and user experience elements for maximizing conversions

Leaky Buckets

Most websites are just online brochures. They're filled with cheesy stock images of perfectly diverse groups of people high-fiving each other or shaking hands. They make unsubstantiated claims of being the leader in their category. If they have a call to action, it's usually something weak like "contact us to find out more" or "enter your details for a free quote."

Even if an ideal prospect happens upon the website, the chances of it being the exact right time they're making a purchasing decision are small. The chances of them actually following through with an action that leads to a sale are infinitesimal.

The situation is even worse when expensive leads from paid ads land on a website only to briefly glance at it and then click away. If there's something that really interests them, they may linger for a while. However, even then, the website will likely end up being one of dozens of browser tabs they have open, most of which they'll never return to.

If this sounds like what's happening with your website, you've got a leaky bucket. To fix this situation, you must be very clear about your website's job. If it was an employee, what's the one most important metric you'd judge its performance by?

If you run an e-commerce store, it may be revenue or average order value. If you run a franchise, it may be inbound phone calls, online chat sessions, or form fills. If you're in the medical space, it may be appointment bookings.

For most types of businesses, capturing visitors' email addresses and storing them in your CRM system for future follow-up and nurturing makes sense. (I'll go into more detail on email marketing in Chapter 12.)

Even if email opt-ins aren't your primary metric, like in the case of an e-commerce store, they are still valuable as a secondary call to action.

Your prospects fall into two categories: people ready to buy today and people ready to buy sometime in the future. Only a tiny percentage, typically about 3 percent, are ready to buy today. If all you've got on your website is a "contact us" page or some other weak call to action, you'll lose the other 97 percent and a heap of revenue in the process. Even some hot buyers in the 3 percent will likely be lost. You need to capture your prospects' details and nurture them.

Plugging the Leaks

Someone giving over their email address is valuable to you—and potentially perceived as risky to them. People are concerned about how their data will be used, and rightly so. We've all been pummeled with spam by overzealous marketers before. For this reason, there needs to be an exchange of value, one where they feel like they're getting a great deal by giving you their email address or other details. You give them something that'll help them on their journey to solving whatever problem they're trying to solve; in return, you get their contact information.

A blockage for many entrepreneurs is what to offer to make this value exchange compelling. Your flagship asset is a good candidate; typically, it would be featured on your home page. (I'll discuss the layout of your home page shortly.)

"Content upgrades" are valuable pieces of downloadable content that complement product, service, or article pages across your website. I've found content upgrades to be powerful tools for driving email opt-ins. Examples of content upgrades include:

- **Checklists:** A summarized, actionable version of the key points covered on the web page that the prospect is visiting.

- **Worksheets or templates:** Tools that help readers apply the knowledge or concepts presented, making it easier for them to achieve desired outcomes.

- **Additional tips or strategies:** Supplementary information that builds on the web page content, providing further insights or advice.

- **Exclusive interviews or case studies:** Real-life examples or in-depth analyses related to the web page content.

- **Video or audio content:** An alternative format of the web page content, catering to different learning preferences and offering a more immersive experience.

- **Discounts or coupon codes:** For e-commerce stores, a one-time discount or coupon code can be an effective way to drive email opt-ins.

Content upgrades enhance the user experience, build trust with the audience, and provide additional value to the web page visitor.

They are typically more effective than generic lead magnets because they directly address the needs or interests of readers who are already engaged with one of your web pages.

The email address of your web page visitor is captured, and the content upgrade is automatically delivered by your CRM system, which gives them instant gratification.

Offering content upgrades on relevant pages of your website and using clear calls to action will help you grow your email list.

Content upgrades are an effective way of plugging website traffic leaks while delivering a lot of value to your audience.

Landing Pages

Landing pages are website pages designed specifically for collecting the contact details of visitors, particularly those landing there as a result of an ad.

When running paid digital ads, clicks from prospects are taken to a dedicated landing page. If you have many different ad sets, you may have just as many landing pages to ensure they're congruent with the ad copy and design. Capturing leads from paid advertising allows you to nurture them over time and reach them directly. Without a lead capture mechanism, you have to rely on prospects to remember you when they become ready to buy, which almost never happens. (I discuss paid and organic content marketing in more detail in Chapter 13.)

An effective landing page focuses on providing a clear and compelling value proposition that encourages users to share their contact information. It uses a strong headline and engaging copy, and it loads fast. An important feature of landing pages is that they use a simple design that removes all unnecessary distractions like navigation bars and pop-ups. Landing pages should be binary in that the only things a prospect can do there are either fill it out or leave. Too many options or distractions will cause the conversion rate of your landing page to plummet.

The opt-in form should be easy to complete, requesting only information that's essential to move them to the next step in your process. While it's tempting to ask for a lot of information on your landing page, each additional piece of information you request will reduce your overall completion rates.

I recommend collecting just email addresses to start with and testing the impact on your conversion rates if you want to request other data. Another way to collect additional data without damaging conversion rates is using a multi-step form. This collects the email address first and then requests additional data in subsequent steps. This way, even if the visitor abandons the landing page when the additional data is requested, you've still captured their email address. You can also request additional data as part of your lead nurturing process.

Continuous testing and improvement of landing page elements, such as headlines, copy, design, and form fields, is important to maximize the effectiveness of your landing pages. I recommend using dedicated landing page tools to help you do this. They allow for split testing, which helps you determine which variations yield the best conversion rates. In addition, they'll help you track and analyze user behavior, bounce rates, and other metrics.

Your Home Page

On a website, "above the fold" refers to the portion of a web page that is visible on the screen without the user needing to scroll down.

The top fold of your home page is commonly referred to as the "hero section." This is typically the most highly trafficked part of your entire website. While you'll have specific landing pages for specific products, ads, or promotions, your hero section serves as a kind of catch-all landing page.

On numerous occasions, I've spent several minutes on a website scrolling and clicking, only to be left more confused than when I started. They often string together a lot of meaningless jargon and weasel words.

I recently came across a website whose home page was headlined "Solutions for Your Long-Term Goals." The description below reads, "Utilizing our core values of passion, integrity, and creativity, we pride ourselves on proactively tackling every project with a solution-focused approach. We exist to inspire positive, radical change in our clients, employees, and profession through partnering and collaboration."

I still have no idea what the heck this business actually does or who they do it for. I wonder how many potential clients and how much revenue they've lost over the years because of their messaging.

This description was obviously written by a committee of jarg-onistas. Imagine being a fly on the wall when they were conjuring this abomination. One guy interjects, saying they should emphasize "*proactively* tackling every project." Several others mumble in agree-ment. Another adds, "Let's clarify that the radical change we inspire is *positive*." Hours later, with scribbles all over the whiteboard and empty coffee mugs strewn all over the meeting room table, they congratulate themselves on a job well done.

Clarity is king when it comes to this crucial section of your web-site. A good structure for the hero section of your website is:

1   **Here's what I've got:** This is the headline of your home page.

2   **Here's how it makes your life better:** This clearly and concisely explains the transformation your prospects will experience and how it will make their lives better. Don't write a novel here. This should be one sentence, two maximum.

3   **Here's what I want you to do next:** This is the specific next action they should take.

Use the magnetic messaging framework from Chapter 5 to ensure the message in your hero section is enticing to your target audience. Here's an example:

Caffeine-Infused Protein Bar

The delicious, nutritious, all-natural snack with organic green cof-fee that helps you crush your workout without the crash.

Shop Now or Get your free sample pack here

The headline clearly states exactly what's being offered: a caffeine-infused protein bar. There's no guessing involved.

It makes our target market's lives better by providing protein and helping them crush their workout, things they really want. We also address potential objections of healthfulness and taste head-on by telling them it's organic, all-natural, and delicious. Lastly, we give them the good thing without the bad thing by telling them they won't have a caffeine-induced crash.

Finally, we have a primary call to action that directs them to where they can buy the product immediately. For the more risk-averse, we have a secondary call to action that invites them to order a free sample pack. Either way, their details will be captured in the CRM system for future nurturing and follow-up.

I recommend using a different, preferably brighter, color for your primary call-to-action button.

Make strategic use of imagery in your hero section that supports and enhances your message. Images of people achieving your prospect's dream outcome are ideal. Also, our gaze is naturally drawn to where others are looking. You can use this to draw more attention to your call-to-action button by ensuring the people in your images are looking towards it.

Avoid auto-playing videos, animations, or carousels in your hero section. They're distracting and scream outdated web design.

Social proof is another powerful thing to include on your home page. Awards, press coverage, prestigious clients you've worked with, great reviews, testimonials, and so on. These reassure your visitors that you're legitimate and trustworthy.

Your About Page

After your home page, your "About" page will typically be your website's second most viewed page.

Someone may visit your About page for many reasons, depending on what business you're in. Here are some of the most common ones:

- Figuring out who's behind this business: Are they legit?

- Checking out your team: What's the size of the team (and business)? What roles do they have there? Do they know what they're doing? Will they be fun to work with?

- For personality- or thought leader–based businesses: Has this person helped people like me? Does this person know what

I'm struggling with, or have they been through what I'm going through?

- For product-based businesses: Where is this stuff made? Is it eco-friendly? How did they come up with the idea?

Your About page is a great place to tell your story, but don't make the common mistake of making it about yourself. No one cares that your grandfather started the business in 1974 or what college you attended—unless perhaps you sell to multigenerational family businesses or help people with college admissions. Then, your otherwise boring backstory becomes relevant and interesting to your target market. Tell your story in a way that's directly relevant to whatever result your target market wants.

I recommend starting your About page with the most compelling thing you've got for your ideal prospect. Is there a big problem or something important that they need to be aware of? Is there an impressive claim you can make that relates to them?

When writing your About page, it's important to focus on the transformation you offer. Instead of just listing your qualifications and experience, consider how it solves their problems. For example, if you're a web developer, instead of just listing your technical skills and experience, focus on how you help businesses attract and convert more customers online.

I highly recommend using visuals on your About page. Include photos of yourself, your team, and your office or factory. Imagine taking the person for a tour through your business and letting them meet your team. Action shots of your team doing their thing are a good way to replicate this.

Include markers of legitimacy, authority, or competence. But again, relate these back to your prospect and their problem rather than making it about how awesome you are.

Finally, ensure your About page has a call to action. It is a great place to collect email opt-ins or direct your visitors to the next action they should take.

Other Common Pages and Features

Other common pages you might include in your website are:

- **Products and services pages:** These describe, demonstrate, and sell what you do. There should be well-thought-out next steps. Only ever sell the next physical, visible action the person should take. For an e-commerce store, this might be adding the product to the cart. For a consulting business, it might be scheduling a discovery call. You'll likely include pricing also. If your pricing is custom or built-to-order, I recommend including a price range here.

- **Contact page:** Give people multiple ways to contact you. Include your phone number if you take inbound calls. If people visit your physical location, include helpful information like a map, landmarks, and parking instructions. Also, include a form that routes inquiries to the right place within your business based on the form's content or a selected option. For example, sales inquiries might be piped into your sales CRM system, while support-related requests could create a ticket in your helpdesk system.

- **Sales pages:** These are focused on converting visitors into customers. You'll typically send leads you've previously captured on your landing page to sales pages throughout your marketing process. A good sales page should include, at minimum, a headline, a problem, a solution, social proof, and a call to action.

- **Frequently asked questions (FAQs):** Answer common customer inquiries. This can save time for both you and your visitor. Ensure these are genuine and helpful, not made up and self-focused, like, "Why are you so awesome?" and "How do I buy more of your stuff?"

- **Wall of love:** A page featuring reviews, testimonials, and overwhelming social proof. (More on this in Chapter 14.)

- **News, media, or articles:** This will be your content hub. Here, you'll provide updates, post relevant articles and videos, and share insights related to your business or industry. This can generate a lot of organic search engine traffic if done well.

- **Compliance:** These are legal compliance pages like terms and conditions and your privacy policy.

- **Live chat:** If you have the team members to staff it reliably, live chat can be a very powerful conversion tool. While many people may hesitate to call or email you, they'll often be much more open to using live chat.

Your Domain

If you're like most entrepreneurs, you've registered countless domains you'll likely never use. I own over 300 domain names. A team member recently asked me for the login details for our domain registrar account so she could allocate them to appropriate cost centers in our accounting system. It felt like someone riffling through my underwear drawer of business ideas and ill-thought-out fits of inspiration. I suspect most were categorized under the expense account labeled "Dumb Stuff Allan Buys."

(I justify some of these domain names as investments because I do occasionally sell some. But most are for my parking lot of future business ideas, most of which I'm unlikely to ever get to.)

The mack daddy of domain names is .com. Despite the recent surge in alternatives, if your customers are in the United States or you serve a global audience, I recommend a .com domain name. I've spent a lot of money acquiring .com domains for various projects, and this can get expensive as many of the good ones are already taken. Some can trade for millions of dollars. In the next chapter, I discuss naming, which can help you find an available or reasonably priced .com domain.

Another option is to append or prepend a word to your company name and use that as your domain name. For example, if your business name is Dunder Mifflin and DunderMifflin.com is taken, you could register GoDunderMifflin.com. This isn't ideal but can serve as a stopgap solution until you have the budget to acquire the domain you really want.

I'd recommend avoiding dashes and other unusual characters in the domain name. These can become confusing, potentially look spammy, and are phonetically ambiguous. I'll discuss the importance of phonetic clarity in the next chapter.

A .com domain name is not a hard-and-fast rule. Successful businesses have been built with alternative domain extensions, but .com should be considered the default. You'll also want to register alternative extensions as a defensive measure. There are now heaps of these, which is quite annoying and expensive, but I usually start with the classics like .net, .org, and, more recently, .co.

If you serve a local market outside of the United States, you should use whatever domain extension your local market is accustomed to: in Canada .ca, in the United Kingdom .uk, and in Australia .au, for example.

> Visit the Lean Marketing Hub to see samples of great home pages, About pages, and recommended tools that will help you implement and maintain website best practices. Go to LeanMarketing.com/hub

Design and User Experience

There's nothing worse for conversions than an ugly, slow-loading, and difficult-to-navigate website. If you're not a professional web developer, I recommend against building your own site. While there are some no-code services and tools that allow you to create a website without a lot of technical knowledge, they almost never work perfectly, and your website will often end up looking homemade.

Even when hiring a professional developer, ensure the following design and user experience elements are covered:

User Experience (UX): Ensure it's easy and obvious to navigate. This includes a well-structured layout, clear menus, and consistent design elements. Watch how people of different ages and technical abilities navigate your website to identify potential UX issues. A website heat-mapping tool can also be very helpful in discovering these.

Mobile Responsiveness: Ensure your website is optimized for mobile devices, as most people now access the Internet through smartphones and tablets. Responsive design will automatically adjust your website's layout to fit the screen sizes of various devices, from small smartphones to desktop computers with large monitors.

Load Speed: Slow-loading sites lead to user frustration, higher bounce rates, and lower conversions. Optimize your website to load quickly by compressing images, minimizing code, and using caching techniques. Monitor this regularly because slowdowns can occur due to website updates, added content, or issues with your web host.

Search Engine Optimization (SEO): Implement SEO on-page best practices to give your website the best chance to rank well on search engines. This includes using relevant keywords, internal linking, descriptions, and URL structure.

Security: Implement SSL certificates, keep your content management system software up-to-date, and use a quality web host.

Analytics and Monitoring: Use web analytics tools to track user behavior and monitor your site's performance. This data can provide valuable insights that can help you improve your conversion rates.

Professional Photography: Avoid cheesy, clichéd stock photography. Get professional photos of your products, your team, and your physical location (if relevant). You'll use these in your other marketing materials as well.

Chapter 9 Action Items

- Set clear KPIs for your website and monitor these regularly.

- Review the hero section of your website. Revise it so it's clear, compelling, and has a strong call to action.

- Take an objective look at your website through analytics and heat-mapping tools to ensure it's optimized for conversions.

10

Your Intellectual Property

CHAPTER 10 SUMMARY

Your intellectual property (IP) is a key asset in building the value of your business. It protects against competitors and helps you drive your marketing efforts.

Highlights covered in this chapter include:

- How intellectual property increases the value of your business

- Why it's important to be careful in naming your business, product, or service and how to do so

- Why standard operating procedures (SOPs) are essential ingredients in your marketing infrastructure and how to easily create them

- Why SOPs and business systems are great investments and the three key things they'll enable you to do

- The importance of style guides to maintain a consistent brand image and voice across all platforms and mediums

- How to create effective barriers against competition

- How to turn large operating expenses into profit centers by monetizing your by-products

Turning Your Knowledge and Skills Into Assets

I've been on both sides of the deal table during mergers and acquisitions. When the business in question had little in terms of intellectual property (IP), the discussion about value was primarily focused on earnings multiples. Just as a product or service with little differentiation will be valued as a commodity, so will a business with weak or nonexistent IP.

By contrast, when a business has strong IP assets, the value discussion centers on what the acquirer could do with those assets and what they could potentially be worth to them. I've sold companies and startups for far more than they were worth on an earnings multiple basis because I had strong IP.

I was able to demonstrate to the acquirer that if they applied our IP to their business, they would get a margin uplift, a competitive advantage, or some other unique benefit. This kind of blue-sky valuation methodology is so much more favorable to the vendor than industry-standard multiples. It's also a good deal for the buyer and allows them to justify the purchase price to their stakeholders.

Regardless of whether you ever plan to sell your business, increasing its value is your main job as an entrepreneur. There are many kinds of intellectual property, but arguably, IP that helps you attract, convert, and retain customers in your market is the most valuable of all. Let's take a look at some of these types of assets.

Naming

The name of your business, product, or service is something you'll need to live with for a long time and is difficult and expensive to change. So make sure it serves you.

Here are some practical considerations regarding naming:

- What's on the label should reflect what's in the can. Be clear, not clever. If you're explaining, you're losing.
- Is the domain name available?
- Are social media usernames available?
- Is it trademarkable?
- Will it infringe on someone else's trademark?
- Is it phonetically obvious?

Naming has two distinct steps. The first is word selection; the second is the construction of the name using one or more of the words you've selected.

1. Word Selection

You'll start with selecting one or more types of words. Here are the main types you might choose from:

- Descriptive
- Suggestive
- Arbitrary
- Invented
- Foreign language

Descriptive words clearly describe your business, product, or service. I like these because they don't need an explanation. This will be helpful, especially if you're a startup, as you won't need to continually explain what you do.

Examples are Cartoon Network, Whole Foods Market, All-Bran, Hotels.com, and The Weather Channel.

The downside of purely descriptive names is that they're difficult to trademark because they use generic terms and phrases.

Suggestive words allude to the benefits, results, or attributes of what you do. They are similar to but less direct than descriptive words.

Examples are General Electric, Sharper Image, Mountain Dew, and The Home Depot.

Suggestive words can be a good middle ground in naming. They can be more memorable than descriptive words and clearer than arbitrary or invented words.

Arbitrary words are real words whose meaning is not connected or only tenuously connected to what you do.

Examples are Virgin, Apple, Dove, Amazon, Subway, Caterpillar, Jaguar, and Shell.

Arbitrary words are distinctive, but in the age of search engines, I generally don't recommend them. You'll be forever explaining that it was just a cool word you liked and then have to spend time, money, and energy explaining what you actually do.

Invented words are purely made up and may evoke some meaning or association.

Examples are Kodak, Xerox, ExxonMobil, Etsy, Oreo, and Sony.

Invented words are the easiest to trademark because of their distinctiveness. Still, similar to arbitrary words, they can force you to devote a lot of marketing resources to making the connection to the products or services you sell. A variation on invented words are words that are based in whole or in part on a person's name, usually the founder. Examples are Hewlett-Packard, Tesla, Disney, and Ferrari.

Foreign language words are similar to invented words but can carry a meaning that may or may not be well known to your target market.

Examples are Subaru, Absolut, Uber, Samsung, LEGO, and Volkswagen.

Foreign language words can help create an exotic feel or an association with something the country of origin is known for. For example, you might use French words for your bakery or Italian words for your fashion brand.

Foreign language words may be real or invented. Despite having no connection to Denmark, American ice cream company Häagen-Dazs invented a Danish-sounding name.

2. Construction

Once you've chosen your words, you can construct your final name in endless ways. These forms include:

- Singles
- Multiples
- Compounds
- Misspellings
- Acronyms

Single-word names include examples like Visa, Oracle, Intel, and Nike.

Multiple-word names include Goldman Sachs, American Airlines, Estée Lauder, and Berkshire Hathaway.

Bonus points for the use of alliteration with multiple-word names. Marketers and poets will tell you alliteration is a powerful device for memory recall and language flow. Examples include Coca-Cola, Best Buy, PayPal, and Chuck E. Cheese.

Numbers can also be combined with words in descriptive, suggestive, or arbitrary ways. Examples are 3M, 7-Eleven, Porsche 911, and WD-40.

Compounds combine multiple words to form an invented name. The most common ones are formed from descriptive or suggestive words.

Some examples include FedEx (from Federal Express), Microsoft (from microcomputer software), Mastercard (from master and card), and Netflix (from net, the short form for Internet, and flicks, a slang term for movies).

Misspelled words can be used to create an invented name while still being descriptive or suggestive. Examples include Lyft, Google, and Krispy Kreme.

Acronyms are formed from the initial letters of a series of words. Sometimes, these can become better known than their full form.

Some examples are NASA (National Aeronautics and Space Administration), NASCAR (National Association for Stock Car Auto Racing), HBO (Home Box Office), IBM (International Business Machines), and UPS (United Parcel Service).

You may need some assistance from a trademark attorney to determine if your chosen name is trademarkable or potentially may infringe on someone else's trademark.

A final consideration is whether your chosen name is phonetically obvious. This is especially important when numbers, dashes, or misspellings are involved because you'll have to continually play kindergarten teacher and spell it out. For example, you have to know or be told that the ride-sharing app Lyft is spelled with the letter "y" instead of an "i." This is balanced against the fact that it's a good, suggestive name with a short and catchy four-letter domain name, which is nice. Obviously, they chose to make this trade-off.

Dashes and numbers can also create a lot of confusion. For example, to visit 7-Eleven's website, you'd have to know that it's the number 7 followed by a dash and then the word eleven .com, which is awkward. I suspect the company might have chosen a different name had it been founded in the Internet era.

On podcasts, you'll often hear sponsored ads where the name of the business or domain name is phonetically ambiguous and needs to be spelled out. This occupies airtime and mental space that could be better used marketing the actual product or service. It also adds additional friction to the call to action, so fewer listeners are likely to respond.

Standard Operating Procedures

As you build out your marketing infrastructure, you'll need to pay more attention to the systems and processes that underpin it to ensure that you get consistent results. Standard operating procedures (SOPs) are step-by-step instructions or guidelines that help you and your team carry out your daily operations consistently, efficiently, and, where relevant, safely.

They're essentially detailed recipes for completing tasks and processes within your business. SOPs ensure your team follows the same process each time they perform a task. They help to maintain quality, reduce errors, and improve overall productivity. They can also be your secret sauce, documenting the unique way you create or deliver what you do.

Your SOPs can be simple text-based documents or include embedded screenshots and videos. My team and clients frequently use video and screen recording tools to create SOPs because it's faster and easier to just record what you're already doing rather than trying to describe each step. This approach lets you visually demonstrate the steps involved in performing a specific task. You can also add a voiceover to your screen recording to provide supporting explanations and guidance.

A centralized place to house your SOPs where your team can easily find them is also important.

Finally, ensure you have a process to periodically add to and update your SOPs as needed. Get team members to document their own work. Sometimes, if you're writing SOPs for someone else, the theory and practice diverge so much that the instructions will be irrelevant or unrealistic.

Your SOPs are valuable intellectual property. Collectively, they make up a key component of your business systems. Systems allow mere mortals to run extraordinary businesses.

For a long time, I wanted to write a detailed and practical book on business systems. Fortunately, my friend David Jenyns has already done just that with his excellent book *SYSTEMology*.

Creating and maintaining your SOPs and business systems is a great investment. The time you take to do so, you'll get back many times over, making your business more valuable. Doing this facilitates the three E's of entrepreneurial freedom—Expansion, Escape, and Exit.

- **Expansion:** Scale your business and marketing operations in a high-leverage way without going insane.

- **Escape:** Have the ability to step away from the business and come back knowing things are running as well as or better than when you left them.

- **Exit:** Many people say they love what they do and don't want to sell their business. That's totally fine, and I get it. While a well-systemized business is valuable to a prospective acquirer, it's also valuable to you because it gives you options.

Trademarks and Patents

Trademarks, patents, and, to some extent, trade secrets can be effective barriers to entry and competition. They become increasingly important as you grow.

As you become more successful, all sorts of opportunists emerge from the woodwork. I've had my intellectual property ripped off in numerous ways. Getting these taken down is a part-time job for a person on my team. Trademarking my intellectual property has made these takedowns much easier. You'll never stop it all, but you can slow it down and dampen the impact.

These legal protections can also create licensing opportunities or be key assets in the event of a business sale. Have you ever seen that simple but iconic image of a yellow smiley face?

It's a bright yellow circle with black oval eyes and a creased smile. In 1963, freelance artist Harvey Ball created it. It took him about ten minutes, which seems about right, given how simple it is. It became a hit. Unfortunately, he didn't trademark it. Franklin Loufrani did and later formed the Smiley Company. This simple trademark has now generated over $500 million in licensing fees.

If your business is at an early stage, applying for trademarks and patents is a balancing act. These legal protections can get very expensive and time-consuming, so I'd recommend keeping them to a minimum until you have traction. I've seen many startup entrepreneurs engaging in "success theater"—work that makes you look and feel successful. Spending inordinate amounts of time and money on trademarks, patents, and peripheral activities while neglecting foundational elements like product-market fit is deadly to an early-stage business. Always ensure the main thing is the main thing.

Style Guides

In Chapter 7, I cautioned against fixating on the superficial elements of your brand. However, congruence and consistency in the way you show up are important. If you sell ultra-luxury jewelry, but your website is cluttered, looks homemade, and feels like a dollar store, you'll create cognitive dissonance in your target market. Ralph Waldo Emerson famously said, "What you do speaks so loudly that I cannot hear what you say." Your visuals and your voice are part of your business' personality and should accurately reflect it.

Consistency is important because someone who behaves unpredictably feels untrustworthy, perhaps even dangerous. Your prospects will feel the same way if your marketing is inconsistent. Style guides help you show up consistently.

A design style guide is a blueprint for the visual elements of your brand. It usually encompasses things such as the color palette, fonts, imagery, icons, and logo usage guidelines. It's utilized in creating your website, print materials, slides, documents, and anything else used to visually represent your business.

Less well known is the copywriting style guide. This is a set of rules and guidelines for written elements in your business. It becomes increasingly important as your marketing team expands. If you have multiple content writers and each writes with a different tone or voice, this is as jarring to your brand as using visual elements inconsistently.

Will your communication with prospects and clients be formal or relaxed? Is it OK to use slang? Will your communication include an element of fun or be strait-laced? Will you have opinions or be neutral? How will emails be written and formatted? Are memes OK? If so, what type? All of this and much more is addressed in your copywriting style guide.

Just as some people are instantly recognizable by how they dress or speak, your unique visual and written style should be distinctive and easily identifiable as your unique brand.

Get sample design and copywriting style guides inside the Lean Marketing Hub. Go to LeanMarketing.com/hub

Monetizing Your By-Products

One of the things you'll notice as you get good at what you do is that it generates some useful by-products. This residue that comes off your business can become a valuable asset in its own right. Chances are someone else wants to do what you're successfully doing. Your by-products in the form of know-how, tools, and intellectual property can become as valuable as or even more valuable than the thing you do.

Amazon has been incredible at monetizing the by-products of its core business, turning cost centers into profit centers.

Their core business initially focused on e-commerce. As they grew rapidly, they developed a robust infrastructure of computing power, storage, and databases across the globe. They soon realized that many other businesses needed this, too. This led to the creation of Amazon Web Services (AWS), a cloud computing platform providing these services. AWS has grown to become one of Amazon's most profitable divisions.

Similarly, Amazon's e-commerce operations required them to build an extensive fulfillment network to store, pack, and ship products. Recognizing the value of this network, Amazon created Fulfillment by Amazon. This service allows third-party sellers to store their products in Amazon's warehouses, with Amazon taking care of the shipping and customer service on their behalf. This service enables Amazon to monetize its warehousing and logistics expertise while benefiting third-party sellers and expanding their range of available products.

I've experienced this in my own business. As part of creating a world-class coaching, consulting, and training organization, we've generated a lot of intellectual property and know-how. It turns out many others want this—we were constantly being approached by people and businesses that wanted to use our intellectual property to start or scale their own coaching, consulting, or marketing practice.

For this reason, we created certification and train-the-trainer programs. This has created a virtuous cycle. We get to help more and more coaches, consultants, and marketers learn and implement lean marketing methodologies and become successful. Through them, we reach people and businesses we may never have otherwise. This, in turn, generates goodwill, referrals, and demand for our end-user-focused programs.

You may decide you never want to sell or license your by-products. That's fine, but thinking about your by-products as potential assets is an important mindset shift.

Lean thinking and a mindset of continuous improvement will help you turn waste and cost into value and profit. You'll see opportunities in places you didn't previously see them. You'll also start to see the inputs that go into creating your intellectual property assets as capital investments rather than expenses.

Chapter 10 Action Items

- Review the names of your key products, services, processes, and even business. Consider if they are still serving you and revise them if they're not.

- Protect your most valuable intellectual property with patents and trademarks.

- Develop style guides and SOPs to ensure your marketing is consistent, high quality, and always on-brand.

PROCESSES

Loose Goals, Tight Systems

"I'll join you in a moment," I tell my wife as I park my butt in that soft, comfy living room couch, laptop in hand. I look over at the clock. It's a few minutes past 10 p.m. I know I should be heading off to bed because I start my mornings at 6 a.m.

I think to myself, "I'll just fire off these two quick emails, and then it's straight to bed." You know what happens next. I visit the nation of Procrasta. The next time I look at the clock, it's almost midnight, and I'm deep in a YouTube rabbit hole. I'm tired and want to go to sleep, but it takes less energy to watch entertaining, auto-playing videos than to haul my ass up, put the laptop away, and take the stairs up to the bedroom where my sensible wife has long been asleep.

Why did this happen? Because I relied on waning willpower.

Just like you, over the years I've tried just about every goal-setting strategy out there—writing them down, visualizing them, sharing them with people to keep me accountable, blah, blah, blah. None of these worked beyond the honeymoon phase.

The problem is they all mostly rely on willpower. Even if you happen to achieve them through sheer force, the gains are usually short-lived.

Here's what to do instead: **Loose goals, tight systems.**

James Clear, the author of *Atomic Habits*, says, "The more disciplined your environment is, the less disciplined you need to be. Don't swim upstream."

A loose goal sets the direction you want to go without being fixed on the final destination because there is no final destination. The goal is to keep playing the game and improving indefinitely. A tight system sets up your environment so it's easy to keep improving.

This mindset is embodied in the Japanese word *Kaizen*, which means "continuous improvement." It's a key concept in lean manufacturing and lean thinking. *Kaizen* is about creating small, ongoing changes to processes and systems that generate significant long-term benefits. It aims to eliminate waste, improve efficiency, and create more value.

The number one reason people are doing what they're doing is because they're already doing it. Inertia explains almost all behavior-driven results. Systems are the secret to harnessing this to your benefit. It's taking inertia by the scruff, putting a leash around its neck, and having it walk beside you like a well-behaved little poodle.

I've made all my most important gains personally, professionally, and financially with loose goals and tight systems.

Big, exciting goals are motivational in the moment but quickly forgotten as you settle back into your inertia-driven routine. Goals are for when you want to win something once. Systems are for when you want to win repeatedly. They give you massive compounding gains over time.

Compound Interest

Albert Einstein once said, "Compound interest is the eighth wonder of the world. He who understands it, earns it ... he who doesn't ... pays it." Naval Ravikant wrote, "All the returns in life, whether in wealth, relationships, or knowledge, come from compound interest."

In a world obsessed with quick wins, easy fixes, and overnight successes, the concept of compound interest doesn't sound very sexy. And it isn't ... at least not for a while.

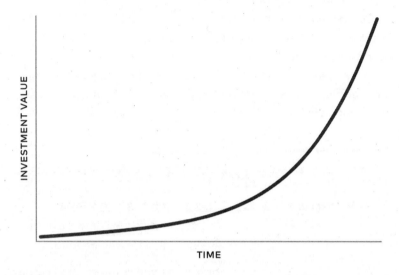

The reason compound interest breaks your brain is because, for a long time, it seems like nothing is happening. Then suddenly, seemingly out of nowhere, there's a sharp turn upwards.

If you put $50 a week into a bank account, after 50 years you'll have deposited a total of $130,000. But if you earn 8 percent interest (compounded monthly) on these deposits along the way, you now have a total balance of $1,718,541. The interest alone is more than ten times the amount you deposited. How did that happen? Through the magic of compound interest.

The S&P 500 historically has averaged an inflation-adjusted annual return of about 8 percent, so this rate of return is not some outrageous, unattainable figure. Anyone can access this with a simple index fund.

Even though this is a virtually guaranteed way of becoming a multimillionaire, most people will ignore it because it's boring and slow. The latest crypto thing or some risky angel investment is much more exciting.

By the way, I love fast, exciting, and risky too! But just as skydiving isn't the answer to long-term happiness, neither are quick wins and easy fixes the answer to achieving long-term business success.

Compound interest applies to every area of life, not just finance. It applies to relationships, health, knowledge, trust, and, for our purposes here, marketing.

In this part, I'll include some powerful tactics you can implement quickly and easily. However, marketing isn't something that's once-and-done.

LEAN MARKETING PRINCIPLE 7:
Marketing is a process, not an event

Your big long-term marketing gains will come from the compound interest of daily, weekly, and monthly processes. And just as it feels like compound interest isn't doing much for your finances early on, a lot of your early marketing efforts will feel disappointing. You'll question if this stuff actually works. You'll wonder whether you're on the right track.

Don't feel discouraged. This is normal. Some things just take time: you can't produce a baby in one month by getting nine women pregnant.

Lean marketing is about doing less but doing it in a more focused, consistent, and intentional way. Rather than doing random acts of marketing and getting inconsistent results, you work your tight system and continually improve it. As you do so, its yield will look like the latter part of the compound interest curve—up and to the right.

Many seemingly overnight successes kaizened their way to greatness, and now it's your turn to do the same.

Conversations Lead to Conversions

Think about the last thing of value you purchased. I'm not talking about a small impulse buy or some trinket. I mean a highly considered purchase.

Did you wake up that morning and just decide to buy? Probably not. You likely did some research. Perhaps you looked at reviews, considered competing solutions, or watched some videos to understand how the product worked or the pros and cons of a particular model. Your prospects are doing the same thing. They're researching your type of product or service—and often, they're researching you.

They'll read reviews, check out your website and social accounts, and speak to people inside or outside your organization. They'll have a conversation about you and what you do, even if it's just in their own heads. A large part of what you want to do in your marketing process is insert yourself in that conversation because **conversations lead to conversions.**

The conversation will happen regardless, so you give yourself the best chance of success if you're involved. You can answer their questions (either directly or indirectly), resolve doubts, and move people to action.

Much of what we'll do in this part of the book will be focused on stimulating and having conversations with your ideal target market.

11

Business Is a Team Sport

CHAPTER 11 SUMMARY

To win the game of marketing, you need to treat it as a process, not an event. Your team is an essential part of executing these marketing processes.

Highlights covered in this chapter include:

- How "Superman Syndrome" is burning you out and blocking the growth of your business

- What to do with your strengths and what to do about your weaknesses

- Why it's dangerous to hire a generalist marketing agency and what to do instead

- Who to hire to run your marketing and how to ensure they get you great results

- Why retaining top talent is the key to your business and marketing success and how to do it

- How to measure employee effectiveness and ensure team members are always focused on the most important tasks

- How to use a "dead man's switch" to ensure you never become a bottleneck in your marketing systems and processes

Superman Syndrome

Many entrepreneurs suffer from Superman Syndrome. There's a problem? You have the solution. There's a question? You have the answer. There's an issue no one else can handle? You'll handle it.

Being Superman is awesome. You feel strong. You feel smart. You feel needed. There's just one problem... that damn Kryptonite.

Here's what entrepreneurial Kryptonite looks like:

- **No one to truly keep you accountable.** Everyone says "yes" to you because you're the boss, and no one tells you your idea is dumb, even when it obviously is.

- **Constant questions and interruptions.** Team members are constantly asking you questions, asking for your input, and waiting on you for decisions.

- **You can't see the forest for the trees.** This often means you're unclear on what to prioritize, or even worse, "everything is a priority."

- **Expensive trial and error (mostly error).** You keep throwing random stuff against the wall, hoping that something sticks.

- **Opportunity cost.** Wasting time and money on stuff that doesn't have a hope of working when you could have been making significant progress instead.

- **Inability to disconnect.** You go on vacation, and even though you want to be present with your family, you spend almost the whole time glued to your phone or laptop, still working, just from a different location. Your significant other is understanding but disappointed.

If any of these sound like you, you're likely still playing the game of business in single-player mode. To be clear, this is entirely unrelated to how many people you have on your team. Some entrepreneurs may have large teams, but the team essentially assumes an assistant-like role. The entrepreneur is constantly required, and lots of decisions and information need to pass through them to keep things moving. This often makes them feel good in the moment, but it's exhausting in the long term, prevents smart people in the team from leading, and puts a firm lid on the growth of the business.

Strengthen Your Strengths

I love living by the bay. Watching sunsets over the water and ships pass by has a calming effect on my life. As I write this, I'm looking out my office window and seeing people engaged in various water activities. Someone in a small fishing boat, a jet skier whooshing past, and paddleboarders serenely floating around.

Because of my proximity and love for the water, it always made me uneasy how bad I was at swimming. I can make it from one end of my swimming pool to the other with a lot of kicking and splashing about, but the energy expended far exceeds the result. As they say, "The juice is not worth the squeeze." Swimming in a natural body of water with waves, rips, and other unknowns kind of freaks me out.

So one day, inspired by a Tim Ferriss article about how he learned to swim late in life using a method called Total Immersion, I decided I was finally going to slay this dragon.

After some online searches and a few phone calls, I hired a Total Immersion swimming instructor. On a Saturday a few weeks later,

I found myself wearing tight-fitting Speedos alongside a hairy dude in a public indoor swimming pool that reeked of chlorine.

He had reserved a lane for our day of training. Some senior citizens in swimming caps were gracefully gliding through the water in the lane next to us. The next lane over had a teacher with a class of young children who swam like little otters every time she blasted her whistle. Obviously, their parents had seen the wisdom of learning swimming skills early so they wouldn't have to humiliate themselves in their forties like I was doing.

Hairy Dude started by assuring me that by the end of the day, I'd be swimming as well as or better than they all were. I'll spare you the details, but six hours later, he was a very exasperated man, and I had drunk at least a gallon of heavily chlorinated water, which I'm certain consisted of at least 20 percent public urine.

Shaken but not stirred, sometime later I decided to learn to sail. I'd become a member of the local yacht club years earlier. It's in a prime location at the nearby beach and gives me access to various club amenities such as a lounge, kitchen, and equipment storage. I like going there to read, write, and relax, and it's away from all the noisy riffraff that swarm the beaches here in summer. As a member, I get their weekly email newsletter dotted with sailing jargon I don't understand, but every so often, they promote a Learn to Sail Day.

After seeing this offer several times, one day I decided to take it up. Again, I'll spare you the details, but I ended that day with a capsized sailboat, a head injury, and almost having my yacht club membership revoked.

I walked away from those experiences convinced that I'm a land-based mammal. I may like being around the water, but I have no business being in it.

If I put a huge amount of effort into swimming or sailing, could I get OK at them? Probably, but it would take *a lot* of time and effort, and the potential payoff doesn't seem worth the cost.

I compare this with the time I took a computer programming class as a teenager. In stark contrast to my aquatic misadventures, I actually felt like a fish in water. I instantly understood the concepts, followed the examples, and completed the work in a fraction of the time of the other students.

With hard work, you can brute-force your way into making your weaknesses less weak. However, nobody cares what you're bad at. Focusing your efforts in areas where you're already strong or have an aptitude gives you a far better return on time, money, and energy. It's also more fun. It usually takes the same effort to make your weaknesses slightly less weak as it takes to make your strengths exceptional.

Staff Your Weaknesses

In the game of business, you can certainly get to a level of success on your own or with a few assistants. If you really hustle, you may even do very well. However, you'll hit a growth ceiling soon enough—if the burnout doesn't knock you out first.

This is why your team is so important. By staffing your weaknesses, you cover your deficiencies, maximize your strengths, and get to play the game in multiplayer mode, which is much more sustainable.

In his book *Traction*, Gino Wickman talks about visionary and integrator roles. Visionaries are the dreamers. They're always coming up with ideas and are natural creative problem-solvers.

Integrators are great at planning, details, and managing daily issues as they come up. The integrator is the glue that keeps the team together and ensures things get done.

Both types are critical to an organization's success. Visionaries bring creative insight to the business and develop new products and ways of doing things, while integrators provide the logical and structured approach needed to execute these. It's incredibly rare for someone to have both visionary and integrator skillsets.

Most entrepreneurs and founders tend to be visionaries. You likely fall into this category if you have many uncompleted ideas and projects. Getting a visionary to focus on the details is like trying to fit a square peg into a round hole. You're taking someone with a weakness and trying to make it slightly less weak. What you really need is an integrator.

It's important to note that the visionary and integrator may not always fall in line with specific job titles. A CEO or founder is not always a visionary, and a COO or CMO is not always an integrator.

Problems arise when an organization is too heavily skewed with either visionaries or integrators. You need a balance of both.

If you're a visionary type, you probably have a constant stream of creative marketing ideas but rarely get them done. You need an integrator on your team who's responsible for running your marketing infrastructure.

The Generalist Marketing Agency Trap

I was recently on a call with someone who had hired (and then subsequently fired) an all-in-one marketing agency, but not before burning through hundreds of thousands of dollars and wasting a lot of time in the process.

The agency spent months on a so-called brand refresh. The result was a cool new logo, a website that served as a beautiful online brochure, and some clever but potentially confusing slogans. They then took truckloads of the client's money and murdered it in cold blood with digital ads that attracted low-value tire kickers. Let's have a moment of silence for that money. It never stood a chance.

I hear variations of this story regularly. Here's how it usually happens. The entrepreneur is busy running their business. They've successfully outsourced some non-core business functions such as IT, payroll, or legal. They figure it would be great if they could do the same with marketing so they can just focus on delivering their products or services. So they hire a marketing agency to do their marketing for them. Feels logical, right? This story rarely has a happy ending.

Peter Drucker famously said that **a business has only two functions: marketing and innovation**. I wholeheartedly agree. These two things are the *core* functions of your business. While many entrepreneurs excel at innovation, marketing is often a weakness.

It's smart to outsource non-core business activities. It can lower costs and allow the business to focus on key revenue drivers. But it's usually disastrous when applied to core activities like marketing. Outsourcing your marketing is like hiring someone to treat your spouse well so that you have a successful marriage.

If you own or run a marketing agency, just hold fire for a moment before you send me your angry email.

The days of the *generalist* marketing agency are over. It's not practical to expect a single agency to be experts in every aspect of marketing. There are digital ads that vary drastically by platform, various social media and content platforms that also vary dramatically, direct mail, copywriting, web development, email marketing, and much more.

Your generalist marketing agency doesn't want to fail you, but they've been given (or have foolishly taken on) mission impossible and, unfortunately, don't have Tom Cruise on staff.

Add to this the following considerations:

- You're one of hundreds or even thousands of clients on their books, so their attention is very divided.

- In many cases, agencies are paid a commission or charge a percentage of your ad spend, so the more you spend, the more they make. This creates a mismatch in incentives.

- When you hire an agency, you're building their intellectual property and capability—not yours. If you move agencies or move things in-house, you're pretty much starting from scratch.

In short, you need to develop your own marketing capability because it's a *core function* of your business. Doing so allows you to take your destiny into your own hands and builds the value of *your* business rather than someone else's.

That doesn't mean you don't hire expert external assistance when needed. That's where a *specialist* marketing agency can be a huge help. I frequently hire agencies and freelancers for all sorts of specialized work. I'm grateful for propeller-heads who spend all day experimenting with digital ad platforms, understanding search engine optimization, and figuring out email deliverability. Good specialist marketing agencies are worth their weight in gold.

However, I highly recommend that routine tactical execution— such as writing most of your copy, creating content, and running your marketing infrastructure—be done in-house. Your costs will be lower, and you'll be able to respond to opportunities faster.

As an entrepreneur, the marketing strategy is *your* responsibility. No one external will ever understand your business as well as you do or care more about it than you do.

If you own or run a marketing agency, the worst type of client is one that just abdicates their responsibilities and then expects miracles from you. By contrast, the best clients come with a well-thought-out strategy, strong assets, and a solid product-market fit. They provide a clear scope of work and have reasonable expectations. Doesn't that sound better than trying to be all things to all people while knowing deep down you can't deliver on expectations?

Don't Hire, Invest

I see many instances where an entrepreneur has built a substantial business through their own blood, sweat, tears, and talent. They've hired or trained all the right operational people to deliver a great product or service, but they still try to run marketing themselves in their so-called spare time, which in practice turns out to be almost never.

They've often been burned by generalist marketing agencies who've charged a lot and delivered little. Perhaps they've done some training or courses but stopped short of implementation. If that's you, you need to hire someone who'll be focused on building and running your marketing processes. If you're just starting to build a marketing team, who should you hire first to run your marketing? Should you hire an experienced "top-gun" marketer or CMO with degrees and years of experience working at a big company? The answer is, "Probably not." They're not an optimal first hire for your marketing team.

Much of their past work experience will usually be irrelevant to your business. It'll usually have consisted of managing internal teams and external vendors who did the actual work slowly and expensively. Some may be a good hire once you've already got a large marketing team and a lot of traction. When you're early into building your marketing infrastructure, you need everyone in your marketing team to be "on the tools" and heavily focused on execution.

To be fair, some top-gun marketers have worked their way up from practical execution. It's the pure managers you need to beware of. Don't get seduced by a piece of paper, a fancy title, or tales of large-scale campaigns and projects. You need someone who'll roll their sleeves up and execute the basic stuff you know you need to do.

However, the biggest issue with someone coming from a large company is that they will likely be set in their ways doing "safe," institutional marketing. Marketing that has no opinion and doesn't offend or exclude anyone. They're used to producing unremarkable stuff that has been sanitized and frankensteined by various committees and stakeholders. They often look down on out-of-the-box ideas and want to play it safe, "professional," and vanilla.

Instead, I recommend starting with a marketing coordinator. This is someone who'll be focused on practical execution.

Whether you're building a marketing team from scratch or adding to an existing one, I recommend hiring team members based on attitude, not necessarily experience. Hire people who are hungry to learn and open to new opportunities. Technical skills can be learned, but attitude generally can't be. Putting it another way, **don't hire—invest**. Investing in people pays huge dividends.

An important idea in lean manufacturing is using smaller, general-purpose machines rather than large, expensive, specialized ones. Similarly, in lean marketing, we focus on tactics you can implement in-house with your team of mere mortals. You don't need gurus, geniuses, or people with one-of-a-kind specialized skills.

Download my comprehensive guide on hiring a marketing coordinator, including sample job descriptions and ads from the Lean Marketing Hub. Go to LeanMarketing.com/hub

Turning Common Sense Into Common Practice

None of the things you want your marketing coordinator to do requires extraordinary talent or highly specialized skills. They'll just help you make common sense a common practice in your business. The key skills you want them to come with are the ability to write, be tech savvy, and have leadership potential.

As discussed in Chapter 5, copywriting touches almost every element of your marketing, so this skill is important. They don't need to be Hemingway, but they do need to be able to write clearly and effectively. Ensure that whoever you hire is a native speaker in your target market's region so that their writing matches your audience's native language or dialect.

For example, if your target market is in the UK, I suggest hiring a marketing coordinator who is or has previously been based there. Even though English is spoken in many parts of the world, there's local slang, lingo, and nuances that only locals will have a solid grasp of. It's obvious when a foreigner tries to pass off as a local.

Similarly, you don't need them to be a tech wizard. You just need them to be comfortable with technology tools and software because so many of your daily, weekly, and monthly marketing tasks will be done with these tools. Technophobes won't do well in this role.

Finally, look for leadership potential because you'll likely need additional team members as your marketing system expands. It's more effective and motivational to grow existing team members into leadership roles rather than bringing strangers in over the top of them. This has three major benefits. Firstly, they'll feel a sense of career progression, which is an important motivational factor. Secondly, they can assist with or be tasked with hiring future marketing team members, which can save you a lot of time. Lastly, having had a key role in hiring new team members will give them a greater sense of ownership than if you just foisted new hires upon them.

I'm a huge advocate of remote work. I have team members based all over the world, including in the United States, Canada, Australia, the Philippines, South Africa, Colombia, and Germany. Hiring remote workers opens up a huge talent pool, even if you run a local business. The best person for the job is not necessarily in your zip code.

Remote work is also conducive to creating a work environment where everyone has a high quality of life. My team members avoid painful commutes, can be there for their kids, and travel without needing permission or time off. They're free-range rather than caged. Many employers worry that such freedoms will lead to low productivity, but trust me, there are plenty of ways to slack off in an office. You'll mitigate this risk by hiring A-players and tracking productivity metrics, both of which I'll discuss next.

Only Work With A-Players

I've had clients and friends who refer to their team as a family. This sentiment seems nice but is deeply flawed. Here's part of a memo Netflix shared with their employees:

> We model ourselves on being a professional sports team, not a family. A family is about unconditional love. A dream team is about pushing yourself to be the best possible teammate, caring intensely about your team, and knowing that you may not be on the team forever. Dream teams are about performance, not seniority or tenure.

I have friends and family members that I love deeply but would never employ. I'll help them in any and every way I can, but that's partitioned off in my personal life. My business needs to run like a sports team and have players who are there based on their performance.

Early on in my business career, I hired people who were "OK." They weren't terrible, but they certainly weren't awesome. They had the skills to do their job but lacked drive, motivation, and ownership. They were B- and C-players, and because of this, many things fell back on me.

I thought my job as a business leader was to inspire and motivate them. The results were fleeting at best, and I never succeeded in turning B- and C-players into A-players. This was very expensive and frustrating. I often felt like I was running an adult daycare center.

Today, I refuse to have anyone on the team who isn't an A-player. I do this for two reasons. First, A-players are a great deal. You pay them more, but they produce much more than they cost you. Secondly, having B- and C-players on your team slows down, demotivates, and drags down your A-players.

It feels bad to get rid of B- and C-players, especially when they haven't done anything majorly wrong and are nice people, but you've got to do it. Your organization will always bottleneck with your weakest team members. You get the standards you tolerate.

Real A-players almost always seek out jobs and opportunities that they're currently unqualified for but know they can grow into. They're driven by pay, for sure, but they're equally driven by the challenge of the role and learning opportunities. If you find that certain people on your team constantly need to be motivated, they're not A-players. A-players don't have to be motivated; they have a high intrinsic emotional need to succeed. They come with "batteries included."

The money you save on hiring B- and C-players, you'll spend many times over on supervising, micromanaging, and motivating them. It's a terrible deal for you and everyone else on your team.

Be a Magnet, Not a Jail

Business is an amazing vehicle for positively impacting the world. You start with improving your own life. Then, your impact crater expands to encompass your family, your community, and your customers. An important group you want to positively impact is your team.

Earlier, I expressed that you should hire based on attitude and invest in your employees by training them with any additional skills they need to succeed in their role. A common objection to this is, "What if I invest all of this time and money into training people, and they leave?" The counter to this objection is, "What if you don't train them and they stay? How expensive is that going to be to your business?"

We've all been customers of businesses whose staff were incompetent. As a customer, this is frustrating, but as an entrepreneur, it's disastrous. It leads to poor satisfaction levels, high churn rates, and lots of stress all around.

So, while it's simply good business to have competent, well-trained team members, to me, it goes further. I want to have a positive impact on customers, but I also want to positively impact the people who help make my entrepreneurial dreams a reality. I want them to take away more than just a paycheck. I want their lives to be better by being associated with my business. I want them to take away skills and experiences they'll carry with them for the rest of their lives.

When you create this kind of environment—where your team is constantly learning and being challenged—they'll do great work for you and won't want to leave. They've likely experienced boring work environments and micromanaging "bossholes." If what you're offering is the opposite of this, they'll want to be a part of it for the long haul.

And if the day comes when they find a better opportunity or want to start their own venture, be generous. Help them in that rather than trying to hinder or hold them back. There's nothing more satisfying than being mentioned in someone else's success story.

Do this, and you'll be a magnet for other hard-working, ambitious, and motivated people. You only need to be a jail when your team doesn't want to be there, and hopefully, that's not you and your business. If it is, I'd urge you to rethink your people strategy. The fish rots from the head down.

The One Thing

Objectives and key results (OKRs) are in vogue in many organizations as a way to measure employee effectiveness and conduct performance reviews.

When I first heard of OKRs, I was excited. It sounded like something that would overcome outdated performance review and goal-setting methodologies. Some skepticism started to creep in when I heard its origin story. My enthusiasm turned into nausea while sitting through a full-day OKR workshop with an executive team. I'll never get that day back.

I wanted to love OKRs, but, like communism, they work flawlessly in theory but falter in practice. The bureaucracy meant to enable productivity ends up overshadowing it, inviting expensive consultants and HR people to surgically attach themselves to your wallet.

Here's a much simpler way that won't require countless meetings and lots of documentation. It comes from billionaire venture capitalist Peter Thiel. When he was running PayPal, he insisted that every employee have only a single focus, and he would evaluate them only on that one thing. Not five priorities or ten areas of focus. Just one. He would refuse to discuss virtually anything else with that employee.

The most important benefit of this approach is that it forces focus on the highest-impact challenges of the organization. Without it, employees tend to focus on easier and less valuable wins. The most important priorities are usually the most difficult or are ones that lack a clear solution. If you give an employee three priorities, most will gravitate towards the less valuable tasks with clearer paths to success.

There are two major objections to this measurement approach: firstly, the need to work on multiple different things, and secondly, it can have unintended consequences.

It's true that most team members need to do multiple things, but there's usually one standout thing that, if they knocked it out of the park, would render their other priorities obsolete. Often, their one thing may result from them doing their other things. For example, if an employee's one thing is the number of qualified leads who book conversations with your sales team, then achieving that goal might involve other activities like improving the website or ad copy and so on.

Unintended consequences are real. During British rule in India, the British government was concerned about the number of venomous cobras in Delhi. To combat this, it paid a bounty for every dead cobra. Initially, this was successful—large numbers of snakes were killed for the reward. You can guess what happened next. People began to breed cobras to claim the bounty, which made the problem worse.

Poorly thought-through metrics will create unintended consequences and perverse incentives. The metric you choose should be easy to measure and hard to game. It won't be perfect at first, so you must periodically monitor, calibrate, and correct course as you get more and better information.

Measuring too many things is suffocating and time-consuming. I love the simplicity and focus the "one thing" metric gives you. It ensures that when you do performance reviews with your team, they will be focused, fun, and devoid of the usual bureaucracy. You can get on with real conversations about their performance and role.

What, When, Who

Cron is an automated scheduling tool used in computer systems to run tasks at specific intervals or times. The name *cron* comes from the Greek word for "time," *chronos*, reflecting its function as a time-based process scheduler. Cron ensures recurring system-based tasks such as daily backups, weekly software updates, or hourly data synchronizations get done. To set up a task in cron, you create a "cron job," which is a simple line of instruction that tells the computer what process to run and when.

Because effective marketing is a process, not an event, I think of it in similar terms. What are the recurring tasks that are going to make up your marketing system? When will these tasks be done? Which ones will be daily, which will be weekly, and which will be monthly or quarterly? In addition to these, you need to account for event-triggered, one-off tasks.

Finally, who will be responsible for them? Some of these processes will be run by automation, some will be done by your team, and some need a combination of both.

An easy way to visualize your entire marketing system is with a table that has three columns labeled What, When, and Who.

Here's an example of what this could look like:

What	When	Who
Reply to comments on all social media channels	Daily	Angela
Write and send an email newsletter	Weekly on Mondays and Thursdays	Jim
Write and mail a handwritten thank-you note	A customer makes a referral	Pam
Send an email asking the customer to write a review	1 hour after their appointment ends	Dwight
Run an educational webinar for prospective and current customers	Monthly	Michael

This "What, When, Who" table is designed to give you a high-level overview of your marketing system and the processes that form it. Your documented standard operating procedures, as we discussed in Chapter 10, provide more detail on how each task is done. Your CRM system will play an important role in triggering, running, or supporting many of these processes.

The Who column represents the owner of the task. Even though multiple people may have a hand in completing a task, who is responsible for it? This applies even when a task is performed by automation. For example, the CRM system can likely fully automate emailing customers to ask for a review. However, even automated systems can have malfunctions or changes that yield unexpected behavior. Ultimately, someone has to be responsible for ensuring each process gets done.

These processes and how they're performed should be tied to each team member's performance metric.

Thinking about your marketing as a process rather than an event is very powerful. This will create compounding returns over time. As your business grows, you'll add more processes to your marketing system. This creates a virtuous cycle that keeps compounding at a faster and faster rate.

The Dead Man's Switch

A dead man's switch is a device designed to be triggered if its human operator becomes unresponsive. It can activate the brakes of a train if the driver is, or appears to be, incapacitated. An extreme example was Russia's "Dead Hand" program, a Cold War–era automatic nuclear weapons control system that allowed for the automatic launch of nuclear missiles should all Russian leadership be killed.

The biggest bottleneck to your marketing success will be you. I've seen this scenario countless times, and I've also been this bottleneck to my team. A project or task gets stuck because it needs my review.

Depending on how much an entrepreneur likes to micromanage, this choke point can prevent something as small as a social media post from being published right through to stalling an important revenue-generating deal.

The business and marketing equivalent of a dead man's switch is an excellent solution to this problem.

Unsurprisingly, one of the processes in my marketing system is regularly publishing content to our website, email list, and other media channels. My team does most of the work involved in making this happen. It then comes to me for review, final edits, and approval to publish.

In the past, if I was traveling or busy with some high-priority project and couldn't respond in a timely fashion, our marketing efforts would effectively stall. We unblocked this by establishing a dead man's switch.

Now, new pieces of content sit in my queue, waiting for me to review them. If there's no response from me after 48 hours, they automatically proceed to be published. This default-to-publish policy means that variations in my schedule don't constrain my team's efforts. Most of the time, I can and do review content prior to publication, but either way, I don't become a bottleneck to the team.

If the team produced work that was way off the mark, this system wouldn't be viable. Our system works because of our detailed standard operating procedures, style guides, and team training.

Chapter 11 Action Items

- Double down on your strengths and staff your weaknesses.

- Work with each team member to identify their "one thing." Regularly review and update it as necessary.

- Identify the tasks and processes where you are a bottleneck and implement a "dead man's switch."

12

Email Marketing

CHAPTER 12 SUMMARY

Email marketing is a powerful medium that has stood the test of time. By mastering it, you'll create a direct connection with your audience and keep them engaged until they're ready to buy.

Highlights covered in this chapter include:

- Why email is likely to be a viable medium for the foreseeable future

- How to get your marketing emails delivered, opened, read, and actioned

- How often to email your subscribers

- Powerful automation sequences that will keep email subscribers engaged

- How to avoid appearing like or becoming a spammer

- How to launch a product or service using a "soap opera sequence"

- How to sell with your nurturing emails without being salesy or annoying

The Reports of Email's Death Are Greatly Exaggerated

Every few months you see another dumb article proclaiming that "email is dead" or that no one is opening emails anymore. Yet when you ask people what their biggest time sucks are, email is almost always at the top of the list.

Over the decades, email has survived abuse from spammers and endured major technology updates. It has seen the rise and fall of many platforms meant to supplant it. Certainly, platform-specific privacy and spam prevention updates from Google, Microsoft, and Apple have created extra challenges for marketers, but email remains a solid marketing workhorse.

Rarely as celebrated are the reasons email is getting better and better. For example, a lot of internal business communications have moved off email onto internal messaging platforms like Slack and Microsoft Teams. This means most emails now tend to be from the outside world rather than internal messages and endless CC chains from colleagues. Also, spam filters are much better than ever before. Technologies like SPF, DKIM, and DMARC (discussed shortly) have made it harder for spammers and improved the deliverability of legitimate emails.

The Lindy Effect is a theory that states that the longer something non-perishable has existed, the longer it's likely to continue. It can apply to technologies, laws, ideas, and so on. For example, if a book has been in print for 40 years, you can reasonably expect it to be in print for another 40. Email is over 50 years old, so it should be good for at least another 50. After all, what else would you use if you needed to contact someone electronically but didn't know what platforms they were on? Everyone has an email address and likely checks it multiple times a day.

While email marketing is powerful, you'll encounter four challenges with it: getting your emails delivered, opened, read, and—finally—actioned. Let's cover each of these and some best practices to improve your chances of success.

Getting Your Emails Delivered

Three major factors affect your email deliverability: technical configuration, sender reputation, and email content.

Technical configuration is analogous to properly sealing an envelope, addressing it, and affixing a stamp so the postal service can deliver it to the intended recipient. Several technologies have arisen over the years to improve the deliverability of legitimate emails and to help prevent misuse and spam. These are:

- **SPF (Sender Policy Framework):** Makes sure an email comes from a trusted source by checking a list of approved email-sending servers for your domain.

- **DKIM (DomainKeys Identified Mail):** Adds a digital signature to emails to verify integrity and authenticity, ensuring the email is unaltered and from a legitimate source.

- **DMARC (Domain-based Message Authentication, Reporting, and Conformance):** Builds on SPF and DKIM. It allows domain owners to set policies on what to do with unauthenticated emails and provides reporting features for monitoring email traffic.

You don't need to be a tech geek to use these technologies. Most CRM systems support them out of the box. But you'll likely need help from your tech person or IT department to get them all set up and configured with your domain.

Your reputation as an email sender plays an important part in how email service providers will handle your emails. Your reputation is influenced by factors like:

- **User feedback:** Email services monitor spam reports from users to help improve the accuracy of their spam filters.

- **Frequency and volume:** If the sender sends an unusually large number of emails in a short time period, that can be a sign of spamming activity.

- **Engagement patterns:** Email services track user engagement, such as open rates, click-through rates, and reply rates. Emails with low engagement may be considered spam or promotional content.

Your emails may be marked as spam or blocked if you have a poor reputation.

In addition to your technical configuration and reputation, the content of your emails will be analyzed. Most email systems will scan the content of emails to determine if they're spam, promotional emails, or important messages that should be delivered to the destination inbox. Some factors they consider are:

- **Language analysis:** Email services analyze the subject, body, and attachments of an email to detect spammy keywords, suspicious phrases, or patterns often found in spam or promotional emails.

- **Links and URLs:** Too many links in an email can be a red flag. URL shorteners and obfuscation techniques can also raise suspicions.

- **Attachments:** Emails with multiple and/or large attachments, unusual file types, and attachments with suspicious names will likely be flagged.

- **Embedded images:** The use of excessively large or small images and images with hidden text can be considered spam indicators.

- **Keyword stuffing:** The excessive use of specific keywords, especially those related to sales, promotions, or scams, can be a sign of spam or promotional content.

- **Content personalization:** Emails with non-personalized or generic content are more likely to be considered spam or promotional, whereas personalized content tailored to the recipient is more likely to be seen as legitimate.

I highly recommend testing your email setup and content if you're just starting with email marketing. There are free and cheap tools that allow you to easily check these so you don't damage your reputation.

Getting Your Emails Opened

Every day, you open your email inbox and decide which emails you'll open first, which ones you'll open later, and which ones you'll delete instantly.

You're making this decision mostly based on the name of the sender and the subject line.

Depending on the email application you use, you may also be shown an icon or avatar associated with the sender and a preview of the first line of the email (known as the preheader). Some email applications might even display the full email address.

Your audience is making the same split-second decision about your emails. So, to maximize your open rate, you'd ideally optimize all five factors:

1 **Sender name:** Using a recognizable sender name helps establish trust and increases the chances of the email being opened.

2 **Subject line:** An engaging, personalized, and relevant subject line grabs the recipient's attention, making them more likely to open the email.

3 **Avatar:** An email avatar, also known as a sender icon or profile picture, is a small image displayed next to the sender's name. This can also influence the likelihood of an email being opened.

4 **Preheader:** This is a short summary of the email content or the first line or two. A well-crafted preheader can provide additional context and entice the recipient to open the email.

5 **Sender email address:** A professional, recognizable, and trustworthy sender email address can encourage the recipient to open the email. The part of the email address before the "@" symbol is the username. In your email marketing, I highly recommend avoiding role-based usernames in your email addresses, such as info@ sales@ marketing@ and so on. Worst of all is noreply@, which, as you'll see shortly, is a massive missed opportunity.

One additional factor to consider is timing. Sending emails at odd times can impact open rates. For example, if you send an email at 9 p.m. on a Friday inviting corporate employees to attend a webinar, it may not be seen until Monday morning. By then, it will likely get buried amongst a heap of other emails that will be batch-processed. However, if you send your invitation at 11 a.m. on Monday, when people are more likely to be at their desks, they may see the new email notification pop up and respond immediately. Testing optimal sending times for your unique audience can help improve open rates.

Getting Your Emails Read

So far, hopefully, your emails have landed in your prospect's inbox and been opened. Your next challenge is getting your email read. In addition to the ten copywriting commandments from Chapter 5, here are some email-specific guidelines.

For starters, consider your email in the context of all the other emails in your recipient's inbox. This doesn't necessarily mean your emails should be short. As per Copywriting Commandment 1, they should be as long as they need to be while still being engaging.

I generally recommend one topic or theme per email. A mistake many people make is trying to do too much in a single email. For example, if your product or service has five unique differentiators,

I'd recommend a series of five emails with a separate email covering each one. If you pack too much in one email, your message will get lost. You want to think like a chess master. If you were playing chess over email, you wouldn't reveal your next five moves in a single email; you'd reveal them one at a time. By making one strong move in each email, you'll have a much better chance of taking the prospect where you want them to go.

Next is personalization. This is where the details you collected in your CRM system are put to good use. A minimum level of personalization would be their first name. You could also personalize the email based on their location, how you've segmented them, or whatever else may be relevant.

Finally, it's important to consider formatting and visuals. Is your message clean and easy to look at, with appropriate use of images, typography, and white space? Use bold or italic text to emphasize important points and improve readability.

Ensure your email is easy to read on desktops, tablets, and mobile devices. It may be displayed very differently on devices of different sizes and across various email applications or service providers.

Typical promotional emails are usually graphically formatted, branded with the company logo, and come from a role-based name or address. They are usually laden with links and images.

Contrast this with a personal email you'd get from a friend. It would likely be plainly formatted, personalized, and come from their personal name and email address. It likely wouldn't have lots of images, branding, keywords, links, or attachments.

Both spam filters and humans instantly recognize the difference between personal and promotional emails. For this reason, I recommend that most businesses mostly use plainly formatted emails. The main exception is for e-commerce businesses, where product visuals are important. I also recommend that emails appear from an individual's name and email address rather than a company name and role-based address. Even though you may be sending to thousands of people at a time, you want to mimic the look and feel of a personal email as much as possible.

Getting Your Emails Actioned

You've done all the hard work to get your emails delivered, opened, and read. Now, what's the next physical, visible action you'd like your recipient to take after reading your email?

I recommend only one call to action per email (although you might repeat that call to action to emphasize it). For example, you might direct the email recipient to click through to a landing page in the body of the email and then remind them to do so again at the end. However, multiple different calls to action will confuse recipients and reduce response rates. Only ask them to do one thing in response to your email.

Directing readers to click a link is an obvious and well-used call to action in marketing emails. This is fine, but a highly underrated response mechanism is asking for email replies. Here are four reasons why asking for replies is so powerful:

1 It's simple and quick, allowing the recipient to reply without ever leaving their email application. Clicking a link usually takes them out of the email application to their web browser, which adds additional friction. This is especially important on tablets and mobile devices.

2 Due to the prevalence of malware, many people are cautious about clicking links in emails they're unsure of. Email replies are often perceived as being safer.

3 This approach transforms email marketing from a broadcast medium into a conversational one, which is much more powerful. Remember, **conversations lead to conversions**—and email is an ideal medium to stimulate these conversations.

4 It helps improve your deliverability. Most email applications will whitelist your address when a recipient replies to one of your emails. Consequently, your emails stand a better chance of bypassing spam filters and reaching the recipient's inbox in the future.

Obviously, if you're going to have people replying to your emails, you want to ensure you and your team are responding in a timely manner and engaging with them in a conversation. For this reason, I recommend routing inbound replies to a collaborative inbox or helpdesk tool. You may even consider email replies to be warm leads and route these into your sales management CRM system.

How Often?

As you collect email addresses in your CRM system, you're building a valuable asset. Your email database grows in value as you keep in touch with your subscribers and build a strong relationship with them.

So, "How often is normal?" That's the question asked sheepishly of both couples' therapists and email marketers. The first and usually unsatisfactory answer is, "It depends on your relationship." When pressed for something more concrete, the answer is: "Somewhere between once a week and twice a day."

The most common reason entrepreneurs don't email often enough is that they don't want to be perceived as spammy. Another reason is they don't know what to send or think they have nothing worth sharing. These are all understandable concerns.

How often you should email your list largely depends on your industry, the pace of news related to what you do, and your relationship with your audience.

For example, it wouldn't be weird to email your list twice a day if your work relates closely to what's happening live on the stock market. You might send an email in the morning about upcoming market-moving news, companies going public, or reporting that day. In the afternoon or evening, you may send a market wrap-up summarizing what happened that day and perhaps some opinion and analysis.

However, if you're a doctor, it may be a little bit over the top to email your list twice a day... unless you have some truly entertaining stories, which, who knows, as a proctologist you might! In which case, go crazy and also make it part of your content marketing.

For most businesses, I'd recommend emailing once a week at minimum. If you email less frequently than that, you run the risk of your email list decaying. This happens when people who opted in forget that they did so, forget who you are, or lose interest in you. This can lead to lots of unsubscribes and spam complaints. All relationships deteriorate without regular contact, and your relationship with your email list is no different.

"If I email often, people will unsubscribe," I hear you say. I'm also the worrying sort, but here's the thing—someone unwilling to give you their attention likely won't give you their money either. Money flows where attention goes. Some people will unsubscribe, and that's totally OK. However, the right people will open your emails, love your content, and buy from you. Also, what use is an email list that you never email? You may not get any unsubscribes, but you won't have any conversations, conversions, or revenue from it either. **The fortune is in the follow-up.**

Note that your emails don't always have to center on you and what you do. In fact, being self-focused and constantly pitching is detrimental to your content strategy. A while back, I had a client who ran some huge massage therapy clinics. They had hundreds of therapists and treated over 10,000 patients every month. Regular email marketing was a key to their success. You might think that talking about massage in every email would get old quickly, and you'd be right. Instead, their emails focused on what was happening in the city that week—concerts, sports matches, events, and so on. Their massage services were mentioned almost in passing, kind of like a newsletter sponsor. These emails are essentially a public service that's genuinely helpful and valuable while also allowing the business to stay top of mind with the audience for massage services. I'll discuss this concept further in our next chapter, on content marketing.

What to Send

You need a solid follow-up strategy after someone opts in to your email list. To do this, your email marketing efforts will include short-term welcome sequences, broadcasts, and long-term evergreen sequences. Let's look at each of these.

Short-Term Welcome Sequences: These are a short series of emails sent to new email subscribers when they first join your list. Short-term welcome sequences serve three purposes:

1 To fulfill whatever promise you made that got them to opt in.

2 To start a highly relevant conversation about whatever they opted in for.

3 To perform automation or segmentation based on the context of the opt-in.

For example, if you're a presentation skills trainer, someone may opt in on your website for a video on becoming a more confident public speaker. The first email in your short-term welcome sequence would deliver this video to them. There are many reasons someone may want to become a more confident public speaker. Perhaps they've been asked to give a speech at a wedding, or maybe they're trying to raise capital for their startup, or they may want career advancement. The second email in the short-term welcome sequence could start a conversation by asking something like, "Are you preparing for an upcoming keynote or presentation?" Based on their behavior or response, you might determine that they want career advancement and tag them accordingly in your CRM system. This could trigger a more targeted email sequence or campaign that speaks specifically to this goal.

Broadcasts: Broadcast emails are one-off messages sent to your entire email list or a segment of it. Unlike email sequences, which are typically triggered automatically by a specific action or elapsed time, broadcasts are manually scheduled and sent. They are used to communicate time-sensitive or perishable information such as special promotions, announcements, product launches, or news.

Long-Term Evergreen Sequences: These are automated email sequences designed to provide value and maintain engagement with subscribers over a longer period of time. They're called "evergreen" because the content remains relevant and useful over time rather than being tied to specific events or promotions. Evergreen sequences can be used for various purposes, such as nurturing leads, promoting evergreen content or products, providing ongoing education or tips, and periodically checking in with subscribers to maintain and deepen the relationship.

Use a combination of all three types, and you'll have a powerful email marketing system. By strategically using these different types of emails, you can build stronger relationships with your subscribers, provide them with valuable content, and ultimately drive more conversions for your business.

Don't Spam

Emailing your list regularly is a powerful part of your nurturing and conversion strategy. Always ensure your email content is valuable and relevant and builds goodwill with your subscribers.

Spam email is typically unsolicited, irrelevant, and aggressively promotional. It's selfish and annoying. It's the polar opposite of what we do in lean marketing. Here are some ways to ensure you avoid spamming:

Consent: Obtain consent before adding people to your email list. This is typically done through the opt-in process on your website, where the recipient agrees to receive your emails. In some jurisdictions, there's also a "soft opt-in" provision that allows you to send marketing messages if the recipient has previously engaged with you in some form, such as making a purchase or filling out a survey.

Transparency: Be clear about who you are when you're communicating. Including your business name and valid postal address in the footer is usually a legal requirement.

Relevance: Ensure what you're emailing is relevant to the receiver. If they opted in for your photography business and you also have a separate footwear business, it would be inappropriate to start emailing them about shoes unless they specifically request this. Relevance isn't just to avoid being a spammer—it's a marketing best practice.

Unsubscribe Mechanism: Always include a way for recipients to opt out or unsubscribe from future communications. Once someone has chosen to opt out, you must honor that request promptly.

Keep It Legal: Anti-spam laws vary from country to country. Examples of laws regulating spam include the CAN-SPAM Act in the United States and GDPR in the European Union. Violating these laws can lead to substantial penalties, so it's important to understand and comply with them. Most marketing CRM systems will help keep you compliant. If in doubt, get legal advice.

The Soap Opera Sequence

As a kid, I got a taste of daytime television during school holidays or the few times my mom would let me stay home sick from school. I'd watch infomercials, talk shows, and, of course, the daytime TV staple: soap operas.

Soap operas had this weird combination that felt simultaneously very adult, very dumb, and very addictive. Regardless of how absurd the plotlines were, each episode would end on a cliffhanger. A loop was opened that the viewer hoped would be resolved in the next episode. Who was the real murderer? Will she find out they're having an affair behind her back? Did he fake his death? Is the baby really his? Will she wake up from the coma? You were always left hanging. Naturally, the next episode would end on another cliff-hanger in a never-ending cycle. Numerous shows on streaming services employ similar tactics, enticing you to binge-watch until the final episode.

Email soap opera sequences operate similarly. The idea is to keep subscribers engaged and entertained by delivering a narrative over a series of emails with storylines, open loops, and cliffhangers. Unlike TV soap operas, email sequences have an ending culminating in some action you want your audience to take, like buying. Email soap opera sequences can be used very effectively for new product launches.

An essential feature of soap opera sequences, as in all storytelling, is hitting on the emotional elements of the story. Each email in the sequence should end with a cliffhanger—an unresolved issue or teaser for what's coming next. This builds anticipation and encourages your audience to open the next email in the sequence until they reach the end.

Here's how an email soap opera sequence might work:

1. The introduction: The first email sets the stage. It introduces the characters (which could be your past self, a past client, or someone else entirely) and establishes the problem or situation. This is where you'll build empathy with your readers. This email should pique the interest of your audience and make them want to read the next one to see what happens. For example, if you're a fertility expert, you may discuss how you spent 18 months trying to get pregnant naturally without success. How crushing it was every time you heard that another one of your friends was having a baby and how easily it seemed to come to them. Of course, like all of our marketing, it should be built on truth. Don't use soap opera sequences or any lean marketing tactics to deceive.

2. The deep dive: Subsequent emails delve deeper into the problem or situation. They provide more details to keep your audience engaged. Each email in the sequence may introduce a new twist or turn in the story. As mentioned, I recommend one topic, theme, or story per email. Remember to keep the storyline relevant to your audience's problem, as the ultimate goal is to guide them towards a specific solution. Expanding on our fertility expert example, you may have an email in your soap opera sequence that delves into the strain the situation caused in the relationship. A subsequent email may discuss why IVF wasn't an option and the implications of that.

3. The solution: The last few emails provide a resolution to the problem or situation introduced at the beginning. This is often where you present your product or service as the solution. You'd encourage your audience to take a specific action, like purchasing a product, signing up for a trial, or scheduling a consultation.

Soap opera sequences help build rapport with your audience by involving them in a narrative relevant to their situation. People are more likely to connect with you when you make them feel something rather than just being self-promotional. A good rule of thumb for soap opera sequences, and indeed all your marketing efforts, is to ask whether it provides value even if they don't buy. Does it entertain, inspire, and inform?

Your Super Signature

Many marketers are aggressive with their email marketing. They try to push email subscribers into buying immediately.

As expressed previously, your prospects fall into one of two categories: people ready to buy today or people ready to buy sometime in the future. Only a tiny percentage, typically about 3 percent, are ready to buy today.

Every marketer is fighting tooth and nail for these hot prospects, paying high costs per click to attract them and then doing a hard sell on them so that they can recoup their ad costs quickly. At the same time, most have poor or nonexistent strategies for keeping longer-to-mature prospects warm. This is hugely wasteful, burns a lot of prospects, and creates ill will.

Of course, you want to address the needs of your hot prospects, but seeing beyond this unlocks a much bigger prize. An important idea in lean marketing is that your long-term nurturing efforts should build value, foster trust, and keep you top of mind with your prospects until *they* are ready to buy. While hot buyers typically make up only about 3 percent of your addressable market, the pool of longer-to-mature buyers can be ten times larger or more. Depending on your sales cycle, these prospects may become ready to buy from you in 30 days, 60 days, 90 days, or longer.

In conversations with my clients, it's not uncommon for them to say they were on my email list for a long time before they felt ready to buy one of our programs. They would likely have unsubscribed and tuned out if I had been spammy and pushed them to buy immediately.

A challenge in email marketing is bridging the gap between value-building content and sales without being overtly promotional. A great solution to this challenge is the "super signature." I first heard of super signatures from Dean Jackson. I've used them myself and with clients to generate millions of dollars in revenue in a non-pushy, value-building way.

People hate being sold to, but they love to buy, and a super signature helps with exactly this.

Get sample email templates, tools, and best practices inside the Lean Marketing Hub. Visit LeanMarketing.com/hub

Super signatures improve conversions from nurturing and value-building emails and drive awareness of your offers. They are placed at the end of these value-building emails and usually contain polite, non-salesy, but specific offers. For instance, your super signature might include something like, "P.S. Whenever you're ready, here are three ways I can help you..." followed by a few offers or products you'd like to call attention to. Each includes a link or call to action leading to the next step in the conversion process.

This allows value-building emails to carry a commercial message without being pushy. The super signature gently guides them on how to engage further with you when they're ready to do so.

As of the time of writing, here's my super signature:

P.S. I personally read and answer your email replies

PLUS: Whenever you're ready... here are 3 ways I can help you grow your business:

1. Get Personal Help with a FREE Strategy Call

Want a second opinion on your marketing strategy? Hop on a FREE strategy call with one of my expert advisors. They'll review what you're currently doing and provide you with a roadmap for marketing success in your business. Book your strategy call at LeanMarketing .com/call

2. Take a Lean Marketing Course

Ready to take action? Learn how to implement lean marketing in your business. Self-paced courses guide you through building your marketing infrastructure and growing your revenue. Learn more at LeanMarketing.com/academy

3. Get Lean Marketing Certified

Help others implement lean marketing by becoming a certified lean marketer. Certification opens up career advancement, coaching, and consulting opportunities. Hit reply to this email and tell me about your situation and goals, and we'll figure out if certification is right for you.

Notice a couple of things in this super signature. First, in my P.S., I signal that there's a real human on the other end, so they can just hit reply and start a conversation, which many people do.

Then, I gently give them three ways to take their journey with me further.

Chapter 12 Action Items

- Ensure you have all the technical factors in place to maximize email deliverability. Work with your IT person on this if needed.

- Let automation do the heavy lifting by building your short-term welcome sequences and long-term evergreen sequences.

- Craft a super signature that you'll use at the end of your nurturing emails.

13

Content Marketing

CHAPTER 13 SUMMARY

Succeeding with organic or paid content is challenging but also rewarding. With an effective content marketing system, you'll create a powerful pulling force towards your business.

Highlights covered in this chapter include:

- Why many popular content marketing techniques no longer work and what to do instead

- The challenges of building a social media presence and how to overcome them

- The five content creator archetypes and how to use them to create compelling content even if you don't feel qualified to do so

- The counterintuitive way to make sales with content marketing

- The importance of a "media company" mindset and how this enables you to directly reach your ideal audience

- How to stand out from the crowd and make content that your ideal target market will find irresistible

- How to succeed with digital advertising so you get a high return on your investment

Fall of the Technicians

I've been surprised over the last few years by the influx of marketing professionals and agencies into our coaching, consulting, and training programs. There was so much demand that we created dedicated program tracks for them. At first, I was bewildered as to why people and organizations who were themselves marketing professionals would seek out our training and advice. As we engaged with them, the picture became much clearer.

Many are excellent practitioners who have already created a lot of value for their clients because of their technical skills. In the early days of search engine optimization (SEO), social media, and digital advertising, technical factors were the key to visibility: the right keywords and hashtags, clever targeting, backlinks, and so on. Many people from technical backgrounds, like web development and IT, entered the space. Their job was to figure out how to game the system so their clients would appear on page 1 of Google, be visible in social media feeds, and interrupt the right people with ads. As people who were used to solving complex technical problems, hacking the algorithms of the major content networks came naturally to them.

However, as social, search, and ad platforms have increased in sophistication, the effectiveness of this technical trickery has fallen off a cliff. Naturally, many of these professionals and agencies are (or should be) starting to panic. Clients are paying them and expecting results, yet increasing efforts are being met with poorer and poorer outcomes. As you can imagine, they're having some difficult conversations with their clients. Many are now astutely realizing the need to sharpen their skills in marketing fundamentals.

Rise of the Machines

Search engines, social media, and ad platforms are two-sided marketplaces of content consumers and content creators. These media platforms have two major problems to solve:

1 Figuring out what content their consumers want
2 Finding relevant content from creators and serving that up to their consumers

To date, the methods for solving both problems have been crude. Search engines used to rely primarily on search queries to decide what you wanted and on backlinks and keywords to decide what was authoritative and relevant. These are still factors in their algorithms, but they have steadily dropped in importance.

As AI and machine learning have started powering content platforms, they've gotten better at figuring out what you actually want, even if your request is ambiguous. We've all experienced autocorrect and "Did you mean?" followed by a guess at what you meant. The algorithms underlying these platforms have become much better at showing you relevant stuff.

Social media and content networks used to rely heavily on overt user interactions such as "likes" or "follows" to determine what was relevant. Now, they figure this out based on behavior like how long a user dwells on a post before scrolling, what percentage of a video was watched, and swipe behavior. This allows them to serve up what users actually want versus what they say they want.

Previously, you could game your way to high search engine rankings or social media visibility. With AI and algorithms powering these platforms, we're reaching the point where that stuff no longer moves the needle.

Your stories, the way you tell them, and the genuine value you create for your audience is now what matters. You no longer need a hashtag or caption to tell the algorithm what your content is about or who it's for. AI has that figured out. Content that's genuinely interesting and helpful will rise to the top, while gameable technical factors will continue to be deprioritized or ignored. That raises the natural question: Is your marketing valuable, helpful, and entertaining?

While search traffic and social media engagement are earned and digital ads are bought, the lines have significantly blurred. It turns out the paid ads that work best don't look or feel like ads. Also, organic content reach can be enhanced with a pay-to-play element.

This is unsurprising given that the platforms owned by Google, Meta, Apple, and Amazon are deep in both camps. They want organic media that hooks eyeballs; similarly, they want ads that won't annoy their users and will perform well. With both organic and paid content, your goal is to produce content your audience wants.

The words of adman Howard Gossage have never been truer: "People don't read ads. They read what interests them, and sometimes that's an ad."

Renting Versus Owning

Most of the marketing assets we discuss in this book—your flagship asset, your email list, your website, and so on—are assets you own. It would be difficult for someone to take them away from you. You're the landlord.

On social media, you're a tenant. You can be deplatformed, shadow-banned, or evicted at any time. You may think you're safe if you're not controversial or political. You're not. Social media platforms are notorious for creating rules that are opaque and arbitrary.

You may be surprised what can land you in hot water. Many have been. These platforms are swayed by a never-ending stream of people and groups with agendas and grievances. For example, many platforms now ban or restrict content or ads related to health conditions, financial status, or other personal attributes. This can be very frustrating, especially when you know what you offer can provide someone with a positive transformation.

In many cases, even spending millions of dollars on ads with a platform still won't shield you from having your ad account limited or banned if you fall foul of their arbitrary rules.

Social media is far from being a place for free speech. Some people like it that way and want it to be a safe space for all, while others feel that social media platforms should be neutral and stay out of policing speech, content, and ideas. There are good arguments on both sides. Regardless, you don't have control over these policies.

As long as your audience is on a platform you don't control, you risk losing them. You may have spent years building and engaging with an audience on social media only to lose them overnight due to a complaint, interference from a competitor, or as collateral damage from an algorithm update. This is why moving or duplicating your rented social media audience onto an asset you own, like an email list, is important.

Another reason to move your audience to an owned asset is because there are fewer distractions there. Distraction is the core product of social media. People have a different frame of mind when processing their email inbox or physical mail. In these contexts, people tend to be more in "business mode," whereas they go to social media to be entertained and to mindlessly consume.

Lastly, social media is ephemeral. Posts liked and engaged with today are forgotten tomorrow. Very few social media posts maintain traction over a long period of time. That's why I invest most of my time and energy into creating quality content on platforms I control. Content I created years ago on my website, podcast, and email list continues to bring in high-value organic leads day after day. I like building assets that can stand the test of time. I then amplify the reach of this work with social media and other rented assets.

The Social Media Treadmill

At the beginning of this book, I promised you that your marketing journey would be filled with frustration, anger, and disappointment. So consistent with that promise, I'll give you the four-step formula for social media success ... but you're not going to like it:

1 Pick a platform

2 Post every day

3 Get better every day

4 Repeat steps 2 and 3 for two to five years

Someone asked Warren Buffett, "Why doesn't everyone just copy your strategy?" His response was, "Because nobody wants to get rich slow." The same goes for building an audience.

Most people who "try social media" won't focus on a platform. Even fewer will have the endurance to post daily. Fewer still will work on improving their craft. Almost no one will do all the above for 700+ days in a row.

Not only are you a tenant, but the rent is due every day. Most social platforms will reward you by boosting your content if you post consistently and punish you by deprioritizing your content if you're inconsistent or take a break. This is because their business model relies on a constant stream of new content to engage eyeballs for as long as possible. These eyeballs are inventory that they sell to advertisers. If your content is boring, inconsistent, or overly salesy, viewers are turned off, which creates a strong incentive for social networks to suppress it.

Social media, when done properly, is a treadmill. This is not insurmountable, but it is very challenging if you don't have a team and strong marketing processes behind you. You want to be deliberate about getting on and staying on that treadmill.

Often, it feels like people with a lot of social media success do so effortlessly and naturally. This is rarely the case. The most successful social media personalities have a team of people behind them. It's not unusual for some larger social media personalities to have dozens of people on their social media team: videographers, editors, copywriters, and much more. Yet outwardly, it just looks like someone with a smartphone, having lots of fun and riffing. Dolly Parton famously said, "It costs a lot of money to look this cheap." This is very applicable to social media. It needs to look and feel effortless and authentic to the audience, but doing so consistently is labor-intensive and challenging.

Many people mistakenly believe that social media is free and they can just dabble a little and get traction. Seeing how the sausage is made makes you think twice. Social media is a worthwhile game and one you can win, but go into it with your eyes wide open, and don't be sucked into how easy it looks.

When you see a celebrity being interviewed and sharing a funny story, they often seem spontaneous and off-the-cuff. In fact, these stories are carefully scripted and rehearsed. Part of the magic is making them feel like organic banter.

Similarly, if your social media is going to be more than just a bit of fun with friends and family, it needs to be well orchestrated. Cute photos of your dog or random thoughts are OK occasionally, but your content needs to be carefully planned and resourced to be a real media channel for your business. If you're just starting to build out your social media presence, you may not need a huge team, but it's unlikely you'll succeed on your own.

Be Platform Native

Each time a fundamentally new platform is created, people try to shoehorn concepts from existing platforms they know and understand into it. This phenomenon predates social media.

The early days of radio were quite different from what we know today. At the time, many radio stations were owned by newspapers, which used them as an extension of their print medium. Radio programming was relatively simple and often involved people read-ing newspaper articles or other printed materials over the airwaves. The early days of television were similar. Many early television pro-grams were adaptations of radio shows, with simple setups focused on news, sports, and weather updates.

In the early days of the Internet, websites were essentially static online brochures. Many still are. But those who understand the medium and its potential use it strategically to capture leads and interact with high-probability prospects.

A rookie mistake many make is treating social media as a broad-cast medium like TV. When they want to get their message out to more people, they just broadcast the same content on more chan-nels. Identical content goes out on Facebook, X (formerly Twitter), LinkedIn, Instagram, TikTok, and so on. If that's your social strat-egy, you won't get far.

Content works differently on each platform. The same person consuming the same content will behave differently on LinkedIn than on TikTok. You need to tailor your content to each platform so that your posts are platform native.

Each platform has unique idiosyncrasies and a "royalty" class that thrives there. These subcultures rise to the top and have a pas-sionate following.

On Instagram, it's "influencers," fitness junkies, and yoga moms. You'll see arty photos of overnight oats sprinkled with blueberries and lots of talk of "self-love." (I'm still unsure what "self-love" is or if it's PG-13.) Everything is airbrushed, and life is a carefully curated highlight reel. Everyone seems to be having incredible experiences and is #blessed.

X is the domain of founders, journalists, and tech bros. Biting sarcasm, shitposting, and wit are its currency. They flaunt their intellect the way Instagram models flaunt their bodies. Contrari-anism abounds. Posts frequently open with the words "Unpopular opinion...," which the poster desperately hopes will be popular.

LinkedIn is the cringey home of HR professionals, recruit-ers, white-collar professionals, and business owners. It's full of humblebragging, fake gurus, and people desperate to impress. A platform where HR managers are rock stars is truly depraved.

TikTok is the fast-moving home of short-form videos featuring funny animals, travelers having adventures, and cute girls doing literally anything. Fun is emphasized and set against the backdrop of trending audio clips and earworms. When TikTok started gaining traction, I thought, "Great, another place to go and watch Gary Vee yell," but it has become a fun platform that algorithmically learns what you like and serves that up to you.

Reddit is ruled by pseudonymous nerds who share their thoughts, feelings, and experiences in excruciating detail. No subculture is too weird or specific. Witty one-liners are upvoted, and endless replies become a stream of collective consciousness.

I know I'm being a bit handwavy. Of course, there are genuine people on Instagram, nice people on X, and normal people on LinkedIn. But, I still keep these generalizations in mind when making platform-specific content. When in Rome, do as the Romans do. So, on Instagram, I share my highlights; on X, I dial up the wit; and on LinkedIn, I add a little cringe.

You need to embrace the dominant energy of each platform. Understanding memes, Internet culture, and the unique attributes of the platform you're posting on is crucial.

I recommend choosing only one platform to start with. The decision to be on multiple social platforms must be made carefully and deliberately. You'll need to resource appropriately so you can be consistent on each.

Social media is not a broadcast medium. Most social media algorithms optimize for engagement so you (or someone on your team) need to actively interact with your audience.

One thing to be aware of across all platforms is that as they become smarter and less reliant on legacy indicators of relevance like follows, backlinks, and keywords, your content will be shown to people who may not have much context on you and what you do. For this reason, make each piece of content as self-contained as possible. You can add context as your prospects move through your nurturing process.

Content Creator Archetypes

So you're on board with creating useful and valuable content for your ideal target audience? Glad to hear it. Here's what often happens next. You're getting ready to write or record something and start having second thoughts. A negative voice inside your head starts intruding with, "Who do you think you are to be doing this?" "Why would anyone read, watch, or listen to you?" "So-and-so is better than you at this and funnier and richer and better looking."

Many people who aren't used to letting their light shine often get so-called imposter syndrome—internalized doubts about their accomplishments, skills, or expertise and a fear of being exposed as a fraud.

You are an imposter if you claim to be something you're not. But for most entrepreneurs who want to do content marketing, that's just their insecurity poking out. Real imposters never have imposter syndrome. If you're feeling it, it's unlikely you're an imposter.

Further, expertise is relative. Compared to your target audience, you are likely an expert. You might be comparing yourself to your peers and fearing their judgment, but they're not your target market. You want to impress your prospective customers, not your industry colleagues.

Creating content in your field doesn't necessarily imply you're the best in the world. Also, the "best" person in your field may not necessarily be the right person for your ideal prospect. For example, Tiger Woods likely wouldn't be the best instructor for a novice golfer because he's so far removed from that level. He could no doubt provide valuable insight on the nuances of professional play, but a novice needs someone who can patiently guide them through the basics like grip, posture, and swing.

The Expert is only one of many archetypes that can create content. If you're truly uncomfortable presenting yourself as such, you can take on one of the other archetypes or create your own hybrid.

Here are the five major content creator archetypes:

The Expert: The Expert is the most common content creator archetype. This person has domain authority through knowledge, expertise, or experience. An important component of this archetype is opinion, insight, and personality. One of the big challenges for The Expert archetype is being too boring and just supplying information. You'll never outdo search engines and Wikipedia as sources of information. Your audience wants your unique perspective and the way that you deliver it. Being boring will neuter your content marketing efforts and make you invisible.

The Curator: The Curator archetype creates a lot of value by sifting the wheat from the chaff. Their value proposition is that they'll save you time and effort by sorting through everything and only sharing valuable and interesting content with you. Media companies, best-of lists, museums, and the news are all examples of curation.

The Interviewer: The Interviewer archetype is somewhat similar to The Curator but is more focused on people and conversations with them. If you don't have a lot of expertise or authority of your own, it's a great way to borrow them and have some rub off on you. The challenge is ensuring that at least some of the spotlight shines back on you so that the discussion is not solely a PR exercise for the interviewee. You want to create value for the audience by asking interesting, insightful, and sometimes even intrusive questions. Look through the eyes of your audience. What do they really want to know? Piercing through the standard rehearsed answers most interviewees have given hundreds of times is the key to success with this archetype. Oprah Winfrey is a great example of The Interviewer archetype.

The Amateur on a Journey: The Amateur on a Journey archetype openly admits that they have limited or no expertise in their field of focus but will take you on their journey to mastery and discovery. They share both their wins and losses along the way, which makes them very relatable and can make for compelling content. It creates a powerful "If I can do it, you can too" narrative. The Amateur on a Journey can take many forms, including learning a skill, building a business, or solving a problem. Tim Ferriss is an example of this. He has openly shared his journey in various fields, such as entrepreneurship, health, and investing. More recently, he has taken on The Interviewer archetype.

The Enigma: The Enigma archetype lives an original, interesting, or unusual life and shares some of it with their audience. Our natural voyeuristic tendencies make this irresistible content. Entire industries have been built around getting a look inside the lives of the rich and famous. While you don't necessarily have to be a celebrity, the key to success with The Enigma archetype is doing cool or unusual stuff that people wouldn't normally get to see. Allow your audience to peek behind the curtain. Reality TV, royal-watching, and people who are famous for being famous are examples of this archetype.

In Chapter 2, I discussed how intersecting complementary skills can help you find a unique niche. Similarly, intersecting multiple content creator archetypes is a powerful way of finding your own unique voice and persona. Gordon Ramsay is an example of a combination of Expert and Enigma archetypes. He has extensive expertise as a chef and restaurateur but also lets us peek behind the curtain of a world we wouldn't normally see. Importantly, he injects his fiery personality and accentuates the drama in what is usually a pretty boring and mundane business.

Archetypes can also naturally morph from one to another or form a hybrid. For example, The Amateur on a Journey can morph into The Expert or The Enigma as they achieve mastery or fame. Justin Bieber and MrBeast are examples of these. You can see their journeys on YouTube, starting with videos uploaded as unknown novices.

You Are a Media Company

I'm constantly asked, "How can I get more traffic to my website?" If you want more traffic, hop on the freeway. You don't want "traffic." You want relevant interest in what you do—the right eyeballs. I'd rather have one relevant visitor to my website than 10,000 irrelevant ones.

Many get into the trap of creating content that will make them look cool to peers and competitors or get them lots of "likes." These are vanity metrics. You can't deposit "likes" in your bank account.

Lean Marketing Principle 1 guides us to create valuable content that serves our audience. Lean Marketing Principle 7 highlights that marketing is a process, not an event.

Applying these to your content strategy creates an important new mindset shift. You start thinking of your business as a media company. Having direct access to your audience has become increasingly important. It's no coincidence that many non-media companies are acquiring or building media assets. This is because paid media channels have become much more expensive and fragmented.

Smart businesses are taking their fate into their own hands. Many of my savvy clients in so-called boring businesses like manufacturing, construction, and retail have videographers, copywriters, and web developers on staff—roles that would have traditionally been seen only in media companies.

LEAN MARKETING PRINCIPLE 8:
Use content to create a pulling force

The product that media companies produce and monetize is content. This is now expanding into every type of business and industry. Treating content as a product line in your business is a smart way of thinking about it. It allows your target market to pull value from you, rather than you trying to push product on an indifferent audience like most marketers do. The right content will entice the right target market—you get what you fish for.

Embrace the Suck

There are a couple of big challenges you'll face in your content marketing efforts.

The first challenge is discouragement. Showing up every day and putting out content but getting what appears to be very little traction can be disheartening.

Getting limited views early on is actually good because it's likely your early content creation efforts will suck. Early on, it's about building the habit of content creation, continually improving, and finding your unique voice.

As hard as it is, don't look at your views, downloads, or numbers at first. This is your rookie phase, and it's going to feel awkward.

Also, remember that your efforts aren't going unnoticed if you have the right value proposition for your audience. You might only get a limited number of eyeballs on a post, but imagine speaking to a small live audience made up of your ideal people. You'd be delighted.

The second challenge is polarization (or lack thereof). Attracting the right eyeballs implies that there are wrong ones. By being attractive to the right people, your content may exclude or even anger the wrong people. That's a good thing. Be opinionated and take a stand for what you and your audience care about.

As discussed in the Foundations part of this book, appealing to everybody is appealing to nobody. Specificity sells, and generality repels. You can either repel the wrong people or repel everybody.

If you're doing content marketing right, you *will* get negative comments and feedback. Guaranteed. That indicates you're on the right track, though it makes many entrepreneurs uncomfortable. They may try to argue, defend, and appease, putting more energy into their haters than their fans. The moment you start arguing with stupid people, you've already lost. As the saying goes, never wrestle a pig, because you'll both get dirty but the pig will enjoy it.

Selling Without Selling

Many entrepreneurs and businesses who've had success selling their products with traditional advertising have struggled with digital media and content marketing. They often get crushed when competing with newer rivals who were "born digital." In traditional media, overt selling featuring the product or service is the norm. On social media, this is the fastest way to have your audience swipe away and ignore you.

When you're putting time, money, and effort into a marketing project, it's natural to want it to lead to your offer, but this doesn't work on social media. Instead, you need to sell in a very subtle and often counterintuitive way. A call to action in each post, like "Check out our new widget here," followed by a link, clearly indicates that you don't understand this medium.

Rather than overt selling, use your product as a prop that's incidental to the content you're creating. Then, create genuinely valuable, useful, and entertaining content.

Think of this type of content more like product placement than overt selling. Aston Martin cars and Rolex or Omega watches appear in James Bond films, peripheral to the plot. Similarly, your products or services should not be the centerpiece of your content marketing efforts. It would be weird and completely break the magic if James Bond suddenly stopped and said, "Go to OmegaWatches.com to buy the Omega Seamaster." Rather, you see it on his wrist as he's choking the bad guy or sipping his vodka martini.

Especially at the beginning of your content marketing journey, nobody's heard of you, and nobody cares about your product. Being advertised to when you want to be entertained is annoying. Think about how many ads you've already scrolled past today alone.

If you sell power tools, people don't want to hear about your cordless drills and angle grinders and how innovative they are.

Instead, focus on building a community of people with common interests around your product. For example, if your target market is hobbyists and the DIY crowd, create content with demonstrations, fun project ideas, and tutorials. These would be entertaining and valuable to your audience, and it's easy to include your products as props. Keep your product in frame while ensuring the content is never about the product. Once you have this community of like-minded people who love building things, I promise you they'll seek out and buy your stuff.

Your business might not be power tools or even physical products, but you can still use this principle to build a community made up of your ideal target market. Leading a community of people who are passionate about your area of expertise is a powerful way to sell without selling.

And just like your product shouldn't be the focus of your content marketing, your leadership in the community shouldn't be about you. People don't go to church because of the priest or the local sports club because of the coach. They go because of a shared philosophy, shared interest, and fellowship with people like themselves. Ensure the thing your community is passionate about remains the star of the show, and focus your efforts on giving them content that's valuable, educational, and entertaining.

Enduring Long Enough to Win

As previously mentioned, getting on the content creation treadmill is rewarding but also challenging. Two strategies can help you win this endurance race.

The first strategy is what Gary Vaynerchuk calls "Document, don't create." Treat what you're doing day-to-day in your business as a documentary. So rather than staring at a camera, microphone, or blank page each day and trying to come up with new content to create, just document what you're already doing.

Initially, this may sound dumb. You think, "Who wants to know about all the boring stuff I'm doing?" Your ideal customers do. I've created all sorts of content over the years, and the biggest hits have been "behind the scenes" stuff where I show what my team and I are doing and how we're doing it. It's also the easiest content to create because we're already doing that stuff, so all we have to do is press "record."

This is much easier for most people than having to dream up content ideas and stories each day. So-called reality TV is built on this premise. It feeds on people's natural voyeuristic tendencies. This can be a powerful content creation shortcut.

The second strategy is to work in the modality in which you naturally have the most aptitude. Some people have the gift of the gab, so a podcast may be perfect for them. Others love creating and appearing on video, so a YouTube channel or vertical video platform is for them. Other people (myself included) gravitate towards text, so written content like articles, books, and text-based social platforms are where they thrive.

Start in the modality you most naturally create in. Note also that this may differ from the one you prefer to consume content in. For example, although I have a daily reading habit, I consume much more audio content because I can do so while working out or traveling. Pay attention to your native content creation modality and start there.

The State of Paid Digital Advertising

To understand the state of digital advertising, it's useful to know its origin story. When the Internet began, it was the Wild West—a quirky group of communities and subcultures mainly run by nerds, for nerds. But soon, online media platforms like Google and Facebook emerged, triggering mass adoption by making everything easy to use and free. Then, they monetized their huge user base. The deal with consumers was similar to the one that funded newspapers, radio, and television—free or low-cost entertainment in exchange for attention. This attention is then sold off to advertisers.

Initially, this was a dream come true for both brand marketers and direct response marketers. Brand marketers had a new place to get in front of millions of people, and direct response marketers had a ridiculously cheap media channel that could track every action. However, their dream soon turned into a nightmare.

Brand marketers realized that their media channels had become severely fragmented. Previously, if they wanted to run a big campaign with lots of reach, they'd do so across a relatively manageable number of newspapers, radio stations, and TV channels. Now, their audience was fragmented across millions of websites, numerous social media platforms, and dozens of streaming services.

Direct response marketers who embraced this new medium early were buying ads for 10 cents a click and making out like bandits as they would arbitrage those clicks for profits. But then they started to be outbid by competitors who were willing to pay 15 cents a click. The next competitor would then pay 20 cents, then 30 cents, and so on. Like most arms races, it continued to escalate to the point where the craziest guy was the last one standing, but the real winner was the arms dealer.

It got to the point where it was very difficult to make a return after paying the exorbitant cost per click. Regardless of what was being sold, most of the profits flowed to Google and Facebook, who became fabulously wealthy by auctioning off clicks at ever-increasing prices.

Since the arms race could no longer be won on economics alone, marketers needed to get smarter. They did this through data. Good data created ways to buy ads more cheaply because audience behavior could be tracked. Another arms race ensued, and the data gathering and tracking became increasingly intrusive. Being good arms dealers, the platforms happily facilitated this and raked it in. When you're on a good thing, the smartest thing you can do is hit the accelerator, and being smart companies, they did just that.

Their core business is selling attention. Already being monopolies, they have no real way to take market share from competitors because, by definition, there are none. The only way to keep expanding their revenues is to expand the market itself. Each person on the planet has 24 hours a day. The job of these platforms is to weaponize their content to get as many of these hours as possible. Every additional minute of user time and attention they get is monetizable inventory. If this sounds like human beings used like batteries in The Matrix, you're not far off. It led to more addictive, outrageous, and controversial content.

As advertisers maxed out on economics and data gathering, their promises grew bigger and bigger, and the volume was set louder and louder.

You've certainly seen this from the direct response marketing crowd: headlines making big claims, loud, obnoxious videos that auto-play, and pushy, hype-filled follow-up.

You've also seen it from the brand marketers, who find new and creative ways of interrupting you and inserting their logos, products, and services into every conceivable nook and cranny.

The party was great until the cops showed up. Backlash from consumers and governments over privacy concerns has now watered down some of the intrusive data gathering and tracking. The platforms, keen to avoid scrutiny, regulation, or even the breakup of their monopolies, are removing many of the targeting, tracking, and attribution capabilities that digital marketers have relied on.

All of this means that digital advertising is complementary to your organic content marketing efforts. It's not the instantaneous solution to lead flow that it once was. Your valuable organic content supports and enhances your paid efforts. At the same time, your digital advertising amplifies your organic content and creates a valuable feedback loop.

By focusing on creating value rather than interruption, your digital advertising has the best possible chance of generating high-quality leads and a positive return on investment.

Digital Advertising Best Practices

Books aren't the ideal medium for delving into the technical details of running digital advertising campaigns on each platform. The policies and best practices of these ad platforms change almost daily.

As mentioned at the outset, we'll stick to timeless fundamentals in this book and point to external resources for the more fluid technical components.

I've included my recommended digital advertising technical resources and how-to guides inside the Lean Marketing Hub. Get access to these at LeanMarketing.com/hub

Here are some best practices that are common across platforms and will stand the test of time.

Hire and Work With Experts

Each digital advertising platform has its strengths, weaknesses, and nuances. If you don't know what you're doing, you'll be sure to mess it up, end up with poor results, and lose a lot of money in the process. For this reason, I recommend working with experts to help you set up your digital advertising campaigns.

As previously mentioned, if you come with your fundamentals already in place, you'll be their favorite client, and they'll be much better equipped to get you a great result.

Always Be Testing

Do lots of testing with your digital ads. A/B testing, also called split testing, is a method of comparing the performance of two or more creative variations simultaneously.

Isaac Asimov said the classic phrase of discovery in science isn't "Eureka!"—it's more like, "Hey, wait a minute…" Testing various creative elements like images, videos, headlines, and ad copy provides valuable insights into your audience's preferences, behavior, and motivations.

This continuous improvement approach will lead to one of two good outcomes—you'll either win or learn. These learnings can be applied to make your digital advertising campaigns more effective but also to other aspects of your marketing, such as organic content.

Ad fatigue can occur when your audience loses interest after repeatedly seeing the same ads. By testing and rotating different variations, you keep your content fresh and improve the longevity and effectiveness of your campaigns.

Effective Use of Retargeting

Retargeting identifies users who have previously interacted with or clicked on one of your other ads or pieces of content. It then serves them personalized ads based on these interactions.

The goal of retargeting is to re-engage, remind, or encourage them to complete desired actions, such as making a purchase or opting in to your email list. This drives higher conversion rates because it targets users who've already shown interest and are receptive to your message.

Break Even on the Front End

The sales revenue you make as a direct result of your ad is known as the "front end." Your "back end" is all the revenue from subsequent purchases. Together, these make up your customer's lifetime value (LTV).

Breaking even or making a profit on the front end means you'll cover your advertising and marketing costs on the customer's initial purchase. Doing so allows you to have an effectively unlimited marketing budget and scale quickly because you're not bottlenecked by cash flow. This sets the stage for you to maximize LTV through repeat purchases, upsells, ascension, cross-sells, and referrals.

Chapter 13 Action Items

- Which content creator archetype resonates most with you? Select one or combine multiple to create your own hybrid.

- Consider which modality (audio, video, or text) feels most natural for you to create content in and select a content platform based on this.

- Leverage your team and create a regular schedule to create content that will be valuable to your ideal target market.

14

Keeping, Delighting, and Multiplying Your Customers

CHAPTER 14 SUMMARY

Many marketers feel like their job is done once they generate a lead or sale. However, the real rewards come from turning customers into raving fans and, in the process, drastically increasing customer lifetime value.

Highlights covered in this chapter include:

- How to get a deep understanding of the experience customers are having with your business

- How to troubleshoot customer satisfaction issues and ensure they never recur

- How to get prospects to trust and believe you by using social proof

- Easy ways to get high-quality reviews and testimonials

- Why most people are doing referrals wrong and what to do instead

- How to use "shock and awe" packages to get the attention of prospects and create goodwill with customers

- How to "arm" referrers so that you massively increase your probability of getting referrals

Customers for Life

Early in my entrepreneurial career, a mentor shared with me his mantra for business success. It was "customers for life." It's a philosophy that has stuck with me and proved incredibly valuable. I've had customers follow me from one business to the next, from my days in IT to my time in telecommunications and through multiple subsequent ventures. Many of them have even become friends.

It didn't matter that I was in a new industry or offering something completely different. They knew I'd taken care of them in the past and trusted that I'd do so again in the future.

What would you do differently if you were creating customers for life? It's likely something very different than what you'd do when you're just thinking about the next transaction or your quarterly sales target.

You probably wouldn't use pushy sales tactics, cut corners, or deliver poor experiences. You probably wouldn't say stuff like, "Sorry, that's company policy." You'd think carefully about how you engage with and sell to them. You'd put their interests first and ensure they always got the better deal.

Regular goodwill deposits are what truly build your brand, rather than all the superficial stuff usually associated with branding. This goodwill "account" grows and becomes an incredible asset to your business. Customers who are raving fans are worth far more than just their own lifetime value because they refer others to you and conspire for your success.

This makes launching a new product, service, or business so much easier and more predictable. You don't have to push, hustle, and sell aggressively. You have a cohort who'll support you because you've always supported them. "Customers for life" is a philosophy that has served me well, and I'm sure it will do the same for you.

Remember Lean Marketing Principle 2: embedding marketing throughout the entire product life cycle and customer journey will make your marketing significantly more effective.

A key to keeping, delighting, and multiplying your customers is to keep doing the things that attracted them to you in the first place. Most customers don't leave because you did anything wrong but because you didn't give them a reason to stay.

While figuring out how to get new customers, close new deals, and make new revenue is fun and exciting, the real money is in the back end—retaining existing customers and increasing their lifetime value. If you're like many of the businesses I see, you can likely double or even triple your revenue without adding a single new customer. How? Glad you asked...

Welcome Aboard

In his book *Never Lose a Customer Again*, Joey Coleman talks about how crucial the first 100 days of a customer's experience are for retaining them long term.

Contrary to popular belief, your customer retention processes aren't something you do later on in the relationship. They should start the moment that the customer signs up.

If you've ever searched for a software solution or service online, the following scenario may be familiar. You've opened several web pages featuring products that may fit your needs. One has a slick landing page with a solution that seems perfect. From the screenshots, it looks exactly like what you've been looking for. They have a free 30-day trial, so you enter your name and email address. The next screen prompts you for a credit card number. You hesitate for a moment, but the page assures you that your card won't be charged until after the 30-day trial. You think 30 days will be plenty of time to decide if the product is right, so you proceed.

You sign into your account. You poke around. It looks a bit daunting, plus you need to import a bunch of data. Unsure of exactly what to do next, you think, "Coooooool, I'll read the documentation tomorrow when I have a bit more time." A day passes, a week passes. Then, inevitably, 30 days later, you get emailed a receipt starting your first month as a paying customer. You think to yourself, "I really need to get on with importing my data into that app."

Another month passes. It's been a busy one. Again, you get emailed a receipt for a service you have yet to use. The problem you were looking to solve now seems less urgent than what you've got going on right now. You cancel the subscription with the intention of resubscribing when you have the time to figure it all out. Of course, you never do.

I've worked with many software-as-a-service (SaaS) businesses, and we achieve big wins by creating a solid onboarding process for newly signed-up or trial customers. If we can get the person who signed up to use the product, integrate it into their workflow, or feel an early win of some sort, then we have a much higher probability of retaining them long term.

Of course, this challenge isn't limited to SaaS or online service businesses. Regardless of what you do, your new customers will likely feel some level of buyer's remorse soon after their purchase. Perhaps the handover from your sales team to your delivery team isn't very smooth. Or perhaps the customer's expectations were inflated and don't match reality. Maybe the penny has dropped that your product isn't a silver bullet and will require effort on their behalf. Either way, you'll get dissatisfaction and churn if you don't have a strong onboarding process.

Do Things That Don't Scale

What extreme lengths could you go to to ensure customers have a great experience with your business?

Paul Graham, legendary investor and the co-founder of startup incubator Y Combinator, recommends doing things that don't scale. This may seem like counterintuitive advice from someone at the heart of Silicon Valley, where rapid scaling and growth is practically a religion. However, it's a powerful way to think about customer experience.

Here are some examples of "things that don't scale" but are key to creating great customer experiences:

- **Manually recruit users.** This could mean personally inviting people to try your product or service, conducting one-on-one demos, or even helping users onboard.

- **Handcraft the user experience.** Go above and beyond to delight your customers. This could mean writing personal thank-you notes and providing exceptional but labor-intensive customer service.

- **Work closely with early customers.** Spend time getting to know them. This allows you to improve your product in ways that create genuine product-market fit. The founders of Airbnb famously traveled to New York to meet their early users. They helped them take professional-looking photographs and handled customer support themselves. In the process, they learned about the common issues and pain points of their customers.

- **Do things that bigger competitors won't do.** As discussed in Chapter 3, doing the common thing uncommonly well can be a powerful differentiator. This could mean providing more customized service, being more responsive to customer feedback, or being more flexible and innovative.

- **Firefighting.** Handle emergencies and critical situations manually. You may not have the resources to build a robust automated system at the beginning, so each crisis can be an opportunity to learn more about potential problems and how to prevent them in the future.

- **Maintain a personal connection with customers.** Even as your business grows, try to maintain the personal touch. Respond to customer emails personally, engage with users on social media, or hold events for your community.

These things may not scale up easily, but they can help you understand your customers better, improve your products, and differentiate you from competitors. As your business grows, you can look for ways to automate or delegate these tasks, but the insights and goodwill you'll gain from them will be invaluable.

Often, entrepreneurs don't go to these lengths because of scalability concerns. Their concern is premature. If you don't master onboarding, you won't ever have to worry about scale. You'll need to worry about survival.

Return to the Front Line Often

As a business grows, it's common for the founder or CEO to get further and further removed from what's happening on the ground. Often, the secondhand information from direct reports gets aggregated, massaged, and sanitized to a level where it's not an accurate picture of what's actually going on.

Want to know what's really happening? Spend a day each month or quarter working on the front lines inside your customer service team or helpdesk. I guarantee you'll be flabbergasted when you hear customer queries, complaints, and difficulties firsthand.

You'll see issues you thought were fixed but are still recurring. You'll see seemingly obvious questions being asked that reveal a gap in your messaging. You'll see the expensive and time-consuming stopgap fixes your customer service team uses because of bad training, broken systems, or poor product design. You'll also discover important trends and be on the pulse of how the business is doing from a customer's perspective.

In individual interactions, you'll find customers who are happy, unhappy, or neutral.

If they're happy, this would be an ideal time to ask for a testimonial or review to use as social proof in your marketing activities.

If they're unhappy, being proactive allows you to address problems before refunds, complaints, or bad reviews seriously hurt your business.

If they're neutral, chances are these are transactional customers who'll be won or lost on price. These may give you a short-term revenue bump but are not a solid foundation on which to build your business.

If you find lots of neutral and unhappy customers, there may be a more fundamental product-market fit problem. Are you selling the right stuff to the wrong people? Or perhaps the wrong stuff to the right people? Is your sales team making outlandish claims just to close deals that your delivery team can't fulfill?

Spending time on the front lines with your sales team is also incredibly valuable. Again, you'll see huge missed opportunities, mismatches between how you think of your product and how your sales team presents it, and real objections from prospects.

Being on the front lines can be a sobering experience. Every business leader should do it regularly.

Fix Fast and Thoroughly

Lean is about reducing defects, improving quality, increasing customer satisfaction, and getting it right the first time. Obviously, there'll be times when you'll fall short of this gold standard. When you do, all eyes are on how you handle it.

Think of times when, as a consumer, you've been unhappy with a product or service and made a complaint. If someone called you back, listened to you vent, validated how you felt, took ownership of the problem, and ultimately fixed the issue, it's likely that this not only repaired the relationship but strengthened it. You felt heard and appreciated.

By contrast, we've all experienced customer service hell, where you feel like you're banging your head against a brick wall and getting nowhere. This is incredibly frustrating. Nothing kills satisfaction levels faster than customer service that's incompetent, indifferent, and doesn't make you feel heard.

It's counterintuitive but sometimes messing up and fixing fast and thoroughly can lead to higher customer satisfaction than if you had delivered as expected.

I'm not suggesting that you purposely create problems to fix them; rather, that you see mistakes as opportunities to strengthen customer relationships. Mistakes are always going to happen. You should certainly invest in minimizing them, but what's even more important is how fast and thoroughly you fix them. That's how you turn customers into raving fans.

Fix It Twice

"Fix it twice" is a problem-solving philosophy that has been a part of industrial engineering and quality management practices for many decades. It's a core concept in methodologies like the Five Whys, which I introduced in Chapter 3.

The idea is that when a problem is identified, you address the immediate problem at hand, which might mean resolving a customer complaint, fixing a software bug, repairing a machine, and so on. But also look at the broader systemic context. Identify why the problem was able to occur in the first place and fix that as well to prevent future recurrences.

Fixing things twice might involve changing a process, improving communication, adding checks and balances, improving training, and more. This can take considerable time, money, and effort, which is why many businesses don't do it. However, this is what separates mediocre companies from great ones.

"Fix it twice" doesn't mean the first fix should be quick and sloppy. Both fixes should be thoughtful and thorough. The "twice" part simply recognizes that a problem's immediate symptom and its underlying cause are often two different things, both of which should be addressed to ensure high customer satisfaction levels.

Prove It

When what you do is seemingly the same as what everyone else does, it can be difficult to differentiate yourself. In Chapter 3, we discussed the four key levers to increase the value of your product or service. These were time, effort, risk, and side effects. You may claim to be faster, better, lower risk, more responsive, and so on, but so does everyone else. It's pretty common for businesses to claim to be the leader in their industry. It's less common for this to be true and much less common for them to have any proof to support their claim.

The problem is, your prospects have heard it all before and don't believe you. Also, they have no way of verifying what you're saying without actually doing business with you. How do you communicate your awesomeness before the sale? You do so with overwhelming proof. Overwhelming in terms of both quantity and quality.

Social proof is a psychological phenomenon where people look to the actions of others, particularly peers or perceived experts, to determine appropriate actions. When people are uncertain about what to do, like when they're deciding who to buy from, social proof can be powerful in swaying their decision.

Some common sources of social proof include:

- **Online reviews and ratings.** If your product or service has many positive reviews, it will be trusted more because it has been "socially proofed" by other consumers.

- **Testimonials.** Testimonials from customers who were in a similar situation to the prospect and can attest to a product's or service's efficacy are strong social proof. "I was lost, but now I'm found" (thanks to your product or service) is a powerful narrative.

- **Quotes from authorities and experts.** Positive comments from trusted authorities, experts, or voices in your field allow some of the trust the consumer has in them to rub off on you.

- **Well-known customers.** Are any prestigious or well-known businesses, organizations, or people using your product or service? Using their logo or likeness in your marketing materials (with permission) signals that what you do is trustworthy and high-quality.

- **Awards.** Have you won or been nominated for any awards or prizes?

- **Celebrity endorsements.** It's no coincidence that celebrities are used extensively in marketing. Their personal brand has a halo effect on the products and services they use and endorse.

- **Measurement.** Instead of just making an unsubstantiated claim, back it up with numbers. If you claim to have better customer service, you can prove it with the average time it takes for customer issues to be solved. If you claim you have more satisfied customers, prove it with a metric like your net promoter score (discussed in the next chapter).

Whenever possible—and it's almost always possible—show rather than tell.

Volume and quality will greatly affect how powerful your social proof is. If you have a few vague, anonymous quotes on your website, that's weak, and most people will assume they're made up.

Contrast this with a "wall of love"—a page on your website packed with dozens or hundreds of high-quality testimonials, reviews, and endorsements. Volume, quality, and specificity help to break down skepticism.

If you run a local business or have a physical presence, consider creating a physical wall of love. Get your social proof enlarged and printed and stick it up. Imagine prospects walking in and seeing a wall covered floor-to-ceiling in reviews, endorsements, and love from past customers. That's powerful.

Social proof can be a bit of a chicken-and-egg scenario if you're just starting out. You don't have a lot of social proof, which hurts your ability to get new customers, and your lack of customers prevents you from having overwhelming social proof.

My first piece of advice here is not to be dishonest and to make it up. It's bad karma, it's unnecessary, and you'll probably get found out. There are two ways to solve this honestly.

The first way is to give your product or service away for free to a select group in your target market and ask for an honest review in exchange. The second way is to ask someone you've worked with in the past for a character testimonial. Even if your work with them isn't relevant to what you're currently selling, a character testimonial can go a long way in establishing trust and confidence in you. People just want to know if they can trust you. Are you competent? Will you do what you promise to do? Your past performance is the best predictor of what you'll do in the future.

Collecting Reviews and Testimonials

Most businesses don't have a systematic way to collect reviews and testimonials. When they do ask for them, they often do so in a haphazard way, leaving the person they're asking to their own devices. This leads to low response rates and poor-quality results. You'll radically improve the quality and quantity of reviews and testimonials if you make your requests as frictionless and specific as possible.

Ensure that collecting reviews and testimonials is process-driven and at least partially automated. Depending on your business, you may even be able to fully automate the process through your CRM system or specialized tools used to collect social proof.

The next thing is to make the logistics frictionless. For example, if you are requesting video testimonials (which you should), there are several roadblocks that the person you're making the request of will encounter.

To start, there are the technical challenges. They'll be recording the video on their mobile device or computer, so they must know how to do that. Then, they'll need a way to send the file to you. High-quality video files tend to be quite large, so they'll likely need to upload them to a file-sharing service and share the link with you.

None of this is insurmountable, but every additional point of friction reduces the number of people who'll comply with your request. This is where your review and testimonial collection tools can be incredibly helpful. They can reduce the number of steps required and simplify each step.

Then, there's the challenge of customers not knowing what to say or write. Under pressure, most people will get stuck on this and won't produce anything, even if they liked your product or service. Or if they do, it likely won't be very useful.

This is where you might give them some samples they can adopt or edit. This is easier for most people than staring at a blinking cursor or camera lens.

Also, instead of asking them to provide a "testimonial," which feels like a weird task, frame it as "feedback." You might say, "Mr. Customer, can I get your feedback?" People love giving their opinions, so most will say, "Sure." Then, ask a few simple questions:

- Why were you unsure or skeptical about buying our product?
- What made you ultimately decide to purchase?
- What specific benefits have you received?
- Who would you recommend this product to and why?

After they answer, ask, "Would you mind if I used your comments in our marketing material?" Most people will be OK with that. You've now made it much easier for them to provide reviews and testimonials—and for yourself to collect them.

To capture this on video in a very frictionless way, you could meet with them using your preferred online meeting tool and simply hit "record." Afterward, you'd have the recording edited to cut out any boring or unnecessary parts and leave just the most impactful highlights.

Orchestrating and Stimulating Referrals

Regular referrals can change the entire economics of your marketing efforts. Imagine if every time you acquired a customer, it resulted in more than one net new customer for your business. Even if only one in ten people referred someone, that would mean one new customer acquired from marketing resulted in 1.1 net new customers.

To regularly receive referrals, you need to go beyond what most people do, which is hope. Hope is not an effective marketing strategy. You need a *systematic* way of generating referrals.

I'll outline three practical ways to stimulate more referrals, starting with the simplest.

1. Ask

If you're not getting enough of something, chances are you have an asking challenge. Asking is the beginning of the receiving process. Yet so few people ask for what they want. They often feel like it lowers their status or makes them seem like they're desperate or begging. The funny thing I've noticed is that high-status, powerful people tend to be the most prolific askers.

On asking, Steve Jobs said in an interview, "Now, I've actually always found something to be very true, which is most people... never ask. I've never found anybody who didn't want to help me when I've asked them for help." He went on, "And that's what separates the people that do things from the people that just dream about them. You gotta act. And you've gotta be willing to fail, you gotta be ready to crash and burn, with people on the phone, with starting a company, with whatever. If you're afraid of failing, you won't get very far."

I think he really nails why most people feel uncomfortable asking. If you don't try, you can't fail (which is my strategy for remaining undefeated in professional boxing). Asking comes with the risk of rejection, and that scares most people to death.

An important point on the psychology of referrals is that people don't refer to do *you* a favor, even if it feels that way to you. They do so for *themselves*. If they refer someone to you and that person has a great experience or gets their problem solved, it makes them look good and raises their status within their peer group.

"Just ask" is simple advice, and as with most simple advice, additional nuance can be helpful in achieving a successful outcome. When most people muster the courage to ask, they do so in a lazy, undirected way. They often offload the logistics to the person they're making the request of. This is the best way to get ignored or rejected by someone busy.

As someone busy who gets a heap of inbound requests every day, I speak from experience. I can give you some good insights into what a good request looks like versus a bad one.

A bad request is self-focused, nonspecific, and adds additional (usually unnecessary) burdens to my already busy schedule. A good request provides me with a strong value proposition and a clear, easy next step. I'll give you a real example of each from my email inbox.

Bad request:

Subject: Article Inquiries

Hello there,

So after spending years and years in the financial industry, I can finally say it's time to follow my dream. You guessed it, freelance writing!

With my experience and creative mind, I have now set out on a mission to create informative articles for sites, just like yours. There are plenty of things I wish I'd known sooner when it comes to financing, and I think your audience would appreciate it too.

If you are interested, please let me know so we can discuss some topics together! I've got a couple of ideas, but I would like to hear your opinions as well.

Kindest regards,

Kevin

I'm sure Kevin is a nice guy, but as much as I want to help him out,

- I have no idea who he is.
- I have no idea how this benefits me in any way.

- In the remote chance I was interested, he's left the logistics of setting up a meeting to me. I'd have to figure out what time zone he's in, when he's free, when I'm free, and so on.

- Additionally, it's all about him. He hasn't even bothered to personalize the email, so I know he's copying and pasting the same ineffective message to many other recipients.

Sorry, Kevin, that's a fail.

Here's an example of a good request:

Subject: You're exactly what my listeners need

Hi Allan,

After seeing your book pop up enough times, and then hearing you on the *Self Publishing School* podcast, I realized your message should be essential listening for my listeners.

I've never experienced such a seamless way to explain the marketing of a business before. All the way from calculating CLV to creating better systems to improve customer satisfaction. I wish I had read your book when I first started.

I've been looking for someone who can dive deeper into these topics with our listeners (consisting mostly of authors in the US looking to build a business with their book) because of how crucial I've found them to be to my own journey.

I'd love to promote you, and the *1-Page Marketing Plan*, on *Before the Bestseller* (a top 2% podcast).

On *Before the Bestseller*, I interview today's top authors such as Mike Michalowicz of *Profit First*, Bessel van der Kolk of *The Body Keeps the Score*, Michael D. Watkins of *The First 90 Days*, Daniel Pink of *Drive*, and many more to spread their message and teach others how they can have impact.

I know visionaries like yourself like to be efficient with their time so I'll make sure everything is buttoned up ahead of time so all you have to do is click a link, answer a few questions, and go on with your day—changing lives.

If you're open to it—feel free to reply or forward me to your assistant for a link to book.

Thank you greatly for your time!

Cheers,

Alex

I did the podcast with Alex. More than that, in our conversation after the interview, he soft-pitched me on an ad management service he offers authors. I bought it and continue to use him as a vendor to this day.

Notice:

- His email was highly personalized to me.

- He has a clear value proposition—exposure on a top 2 percent podcast.

- He gave me social proof. My peers have appeared on this same podcast.

- He made it clear he wouldn't waste my time. I can't tell you how often I've regretted meeting with someone who was disorganized and inconsiderate of my schedule.

- He made the ask very clear.

- He made the next step clear and the logistics easy. All I had to do was forward the email to my assistant, who took care of the rest with him.

- Additional points for appealing to my ego. Who doesn't like being told they're awesome?

2. Make It Part of Your Product

Another reason referral requests sometimes fall flat is because they come unexpectedly, and the person receiving the request is caught off guard. Often, your customer may have someone in their life they can refer to you, but they're just not currently top of mind. They may need to think about it or come across them in their day-to-day dealings. If you catch them off guard with a referral request, their natural tendency will be to say, "I can't think of anyone at the moment."

As discussed earlier, you'll set clear expectations in your onboarding process. So set the expectation there, or possibly even in your sales process, that referrals are a normal part of working with you. If possible and appropriate, make this a two-way street where you'll also send referrals to them.

I'm often asked about incentivizing referrals. Over the years, I've made countless high-, low-, and medium-value referrals. I can't recall a single instance where an incentive or bounty was my motivator. Even when it was offered afterward, I've turned it down. I'm not saying referrals don't happen this way, but I think it's much less common than most entrepreneurs think.

This has to do with the psychology of referrals. The real payoff most referrers get is not from your kickback, incentive, or trinket. It's the social payoff of raising their status within their peer group. By referring someone in their peer group to something valuable, that value gets associated with them. Getting a direct payoff with an incentive kills this. Even worse, it can lower their status within their peer group because the person they refer might (and probably will) find out the referral was incentivized.

If your friend referred you to a financial advisor and you found out later on they had been incentivized, wouldn't you at least wonder if their motivation was genuine or selfish?

Of course, the situation is completely different when there's a formal referral relationship, such as in a joint venture, affiliate program, or reseller arrangement. In these cases, it forms a core part of the business model. I know my insurance broker gets paid by the insurer for his recommendations to me and I'm OK with that. In many instances, disclosure of incentives and payments is a legal requirement. This is particularly important in fields where conflicts of interest could influence professional judgment, such as real estate, finance, and healthcare. In some cases, incentivized referrals are even illegal.

A way to really put a rocket under organic referrals is if your product or service gets better for both the referrer and referee if they both use it. This is called a network effect.

For example, a social network or communications platform becomes much more valuable to you if all your friends are on it. In turn, it becomes valuable to them to have their other friends on it. This creates inherent virality. You win, your friends win, and the platform wins. It's not always easy or possible to build network effects into your product or service, but the payoff is huge if you can.

3. Arm Your Referrers

Most people's requests for referrals are vague and self-focused and place a burden on the potential referrer. It's usually something like, "If you know someone who needs an IT managed service provider, please let them know about us."

Who would be a good fit? How would I let them know about you? What should they do? What indicators should I look for that tell me they're ready to buy? These may seem like stupidly obvious questions, and maybe for some simpler businesses, they are, but either way, you're still forcing potential referrers to do all the work for you. Unless they're highly motivated, they probably won't.

If you were the commander of an army, you wouldn't send your soldiers into battle unarmed and expect them to come back to you with the spoils of war. It's nice when miracles happen, but they tend to happen more reliably when you create favorable circumstances for them. We want our referrers to conquer on our behalf, so let's arm them also.

As expressed earlier, the key to unlocking referrals is understanding the core psychology behind why people make them. Outside your inner circle of friends and family, no one is referring business to you out of benevolence.

With this in mind, your most reliable path to orchestrating and stimulating referrals is arming your referrer with an asset they can pass on. This makes them look and feel good within their peer group.

This also helps stimulate referrals you otherwise wouldn't have received, because most people will only make a referral to someone they know is hot, ready to buy, and a perfect fit. If they're unsure of willingness, intention, or fit, most people will err on the side of caution and won't risk making an unsuitable referral. However, passing on an asset is a low-risk way for them to introduce what you do because it doesn't create obligation or sales pressure.

I like arming referrers with assets that have inherent value. Firstly, throwing them out feels extremely wasteful, so recipients typically keep them or pass them on to someone else. Secondly, it raises the status of the referrer because they're giving a valuable gift rather than just making a referral.

In my business, when we're working with a partner or potential referrer, we'll give them copies of my books to pass on to their community. Books almost never get thrown out, and recipients appreciate the gift, both for the intrinsic value and the value of the content. It's a great way to introduce them to our world and, importantly, elevate the status of the referrer.

A voucher or gift card with a value that can be redeemed for your products or services is another excellent way to arm your referrers. You could even mimic the design of commercial gift cards, which typically have the same dimensions as a credit card and a face value printed on them. Everyone has a wallet full of plastic cards that they associate with value and fear to lose.

A sampler pack, taster version, or starter kit can work well if you sell physical products. Depending on what it is, your flagship asset may also be a great way to arm your referral network.

Gifting

Gifting is a great way to solidify relationships and make customers feel seen and appreciated. However, most people do gifting terribly. To do gifting well, you need to be thoughtful and a bit contrarian.

For starters, skip all the major holidays. Your gesture will be lost in the crowd with everyone else's gifts, greetings, and well wishes.

Also, skip the cheap plastic pens or other trinkets with your company name and logo plastered all over them. That's not a gift for your customer. That's an advertisement and not a very good one.

In *Influence*, Robert Cialdini highlights how the principle of reciprocity is triggered when gifts are meaningful, unexpected, and customized.

Meaningful means the gift should have some level of importance or significance to the recipient. It's not about the financial value of the gift but rather its perceived value and meaning to the recipient.

Unexpected gifts have a strong impact because the element of surprise can evoke stronger emotions and be more memorable.

A customized or personalized gift demonstrates that the giver has put thought into it and makes the recipient feel special and recognized as an individual rather than just part of a mass marketing strategy.

John Ruhlin, author of *Giftology*, recommends that your gift be best-in-class for whatever budget you have allocated. So, for example, if you have a $100 budget per client, rather than gifting them a cheap plastic watch that they'll give away or throw out, give them a beautiful, high-quality pen with their name engraved on it. The last point is an important one. The gift should have *their* name on it rather than your company name or logo. A high-quality gift with their own name on it will likely be kept forever and remind them of you with each use.

It's important to make gifting a consistent practice rather than a one-off gesture. Like all marketing processes, the power of gifting compounds over time and helps sustain and strengthen customer relationships.

Shock and Awe with Snail Mail

Have you ever received a package and thrown it away before opening it? Neither have I. I think it would be fair to assume that packages have as close to a 100 percent open rate as you can possibly get.

Sending a physical package or mail has the potential to deliver outsized results. As a tech geek by nature, I love the digital world. However, as digital inboxes have gotten increasingly crowded over the years, physical inboxes have become clearer and cleaner. As a marketer, that's hard to ignore.

With digital marketing costs rising sharply in certain industries and markets, I've found many instances where it's actually cheaper to mail someone a package, perhaps with a sample product or handwritten note, than it is to get them to pay attention through purely digital mediums.

As a marketer, you want to show up in ways and places that create a pattern interrupt. Whether it's stopping the scroll online or showing up in their physical world with something as simple as a handwritten note, you want to create a "wow" moment.

A "shock and awe" package is a physical mail package sent (often unexpectedly) to prospects, customers, or potential partners. The package might include:

- A personalized letter or handwritten note

- High-quality promotional materials

- Testimonials and social proof

- Books or special reports

- Product samples or demonstrations

- High-quality gifts

The idea behind the shock and awe package is to create a sense of overwhelming value in the eyes of the recipient. It can position the sender as an expert and create tremendous goodwill when done well.

This approach is especially effective in industries where differentiation can be challenging. Instead of being just another voice in a crowded marketplace, the shock and awe package allows you to stand out and make a lasting impression.

Expectations, Quick Wins, and Roadmaps

If what you do takes time to deliver or to get your customers the result they want, you'll likely have a challenge with customer satisfaction and retention. People get impatient and sometimes even cancel, quit, or churn before you've had a chance to help them through a transformation. This is particularly challenging in fields like consulting, healthcare, fitness, and education, where getting a result relies heavily on the customer continuing to do the things they need to do. It's frustrating to see someone who was making progress give up before they got their big payoff. Here are three things you can do to tackle this head-on—set clear expectations, create quick wins, and provide a roadmap.

Set Clear Expectations: Just before the sale is made, everyone's excited. The customer is excited about the transformation that will happen in their business or life, and your sales team is excited because they're just about to close a new deal. This can create unrealistic expectations, either because the sales team overpromises or because the customer was left to imagine how fast and easily they'd get the desired outcome. Often, it's a combination of both.

Either way, this is a huge problem that will come back to bite you and damage your customer lifetime value (LTV). (I'll discuss LTV further in the next chapter.) It's essential that your sales team clearly sets out how long it will take and how hard it will be for the customer to get the outcome they want. This kind of transparency will actually be *attractive* to the right customer.

I would strongly caution you against taking "desperate money." These are people who are willing to buy, but it's their final roll of the dice, and they're highly unlikely to succeed. It's bad from an ethical point of view, it's bad for LTV, and it's bad for you and your team's sanity. It also leads to bad reviews, unhappy customers, and refunds. These are headaches you don't need.

Create Quick Wins: Even the right customer can get discouraged if they're not feeling a sense of progress after a while. Engineer ways that they can get some wins early on in their journey and throughout their time with you.

For example, if you teach a musical instrument, the student may take a long time to become proficient. You could give them a quick win and make them feel more competent by teaching them simple, recognizable tunes they can play for friends and family, like "Twinkle, Twinkle, Little Star" or "Happy Birthday."

There's a danger that customers get hooked on quick wins and become short-term-focused, so you should clearly communicate that this is a quick win along a much bigger journey.

In some businesses and industries, there's a big gap between the time the order is taken and when it's delivered. For example, back in the day, I used to own a telecommunications company. After our sales team got a completed order from the customer, it could be a few weeks before we could deliver service to them. We were often waiting for third-party technicians, upstream telecom companies, and hardware to arrive.

Even when the sales team clearly set the time expectation, we'd often hear back from customers asking about the status of their order. Uncertainty creeps in when there's no communication, and customers feel like nothing is happening. We implemented a simple communications process called a "no news update." Basically, they'd hear from us every few days even if there was nothing new to communicate. We'd include some tidbit of information and assure them that everything was on track. Things like "we've received your order" or "your equipment is on the way" and so on. Satisfaction levels dramatically increased as customers felt looped in and knew that their order wasn't lost in some black hole.

Provide a Roadmap: If you've ever been lost in a mall or on a hike, the map that tells you "you are here" in the context of the bigger picture can be a godsend. Similarly, I recommend you create a visual roadmap of all the major milestones in the journey you'll take your customer on. This may look somewhat like a flow chart, but I recommend you put some time and effort into making it more graphical and visually appealing. When we did this in my business, it was a game changer.

You can use roadmaps in a few different ways. The first way is on sales calls. Particularly if you sell something invisible like consulting or training, showing the journey visually is powerful. It's also helpful in setting expectations.

The second way we use roadmaps is throughout the customer journey. Showing customers "you are here" in the context of the transformation they're working towards keeps the momentum and motivation going.

Another reason I like roadmaps both in the sales process and throughout the customer journey is because they show that you and your team have a structured process. You're not just winging it and making things up as you go along. As a customer of various coaches, consultants, and trainers over the years, I've often found myself wondering, "Where is this going? Does this person have a plan? Am I on track?" A roadmap would have gone a long way to alleviating my anxiety and giving me confidence in the person or program.

Chapter 14 Action Items

- Spend some time each month embedded inside your customer service team or helpdesk to understand your customers at a deeper level.

- Arm your customers and referral network with a valuable asset that they can pass on.

- Create a process that makes it easy for customers to give you reviews and testimonials.

15

Metrics

CHAPTER 15 SUMMARY

Most marketing campaigns won't achieve immediate success. While this can be discouraging, having a systematic troubleshooting approach, taking corrective action, and understanding key metrics will help you achieve long-term profitability.

Highlights covered in this chapter include:

- The practice of continuous improvement at each step in your marketing campaigns

- How to troubleshoot an advertising campaign that isn't working

- Why it's important to track leading and lagging metrics and how to do so

- The one marketing metric that matters above all others

- The critical metrics for subscription-based businesses

- The micrometrics that can help you track the success of your marketing campaigns

- Why it's important to view your analytics from both zoomed-in and zoomed-out perspectives

Most People Won't

It's easy to get discouraged when your marketing efforts don't seem to be paying off. We all want to see our metrics trending sharply upward. We want everyone to know how awesome we are and pay attention. But the reality is, most people won't.

Most people won't click your ad. Most of the people who click your ad won't opt in. Most of the people who opt in won't open your email. Most of the people who open the email won't click the link to your sales page. Most of the people who click through to your sales page won't click through to the order form. Most of the people who click through to the order form won't complete the order.

This doesn't mean your product is bad or your marketing is broken. It's normal. If most people did, your conversion rates would be over 50 percent. You'd be the most brilliant person in the history of marketing. They would have a gold statue of you on Madison Avenue.

I introduced the midwit at the beginning of this book. A common phrase you'll hear from midwits is, "I tried it, and it didn't work." What they're really saying is, "I tried it once half-heartedly and never bothered figuring out where I messed it up along the way."

Almost anything you start won't work as well as you hoped initially. That's life doing its thing.

In marketing, you'll often hear midwits say things like, "Marketing doesn't work in my industry" or "Advertising is a waste of money."

Can you imagine someone in manufacturing saying, "I tried manufacturing, but it didn't work"? Wouldn't the next logical question you'd ask them be, "What specifically didn't work?"

In lean manufacturing, when an assembly line worker identifies an issue in the production process, such as a defect, missing part, or unsafe condition, they immediately pull the Andon cord. This stops the production line, lights up a board, and notifies supervisors, team leaders, or maintenance personnel.

An analysis is done to identify the root cause of the issue, and a fix is implemented. The production line is then restarted. As you can imagine, things get better fast.

You should do the same with your marketing.

LEAN MARKETING PRINCIPLE 9:
Test, measure, and continuously improve each step in your marketing campaigns

For example, if your paid digital ad campaign isn't performing, the lean marketing way is to pull the metaphorical Andon cord and troubleshoot. You need to figure out exactly which step isn't converting as well as you want it to.

The good news is there are only a few things that could be going on:

1 They're not clicking on the ad

2 They're not opting in

3 They're opting in but either not getting or not opening your email

4 They're opening your email but not going to your sales page

5 They're going to your sales page but not buying

These are the only possibilities. So saying "I tried it, and it didn't work" doesn't make sense.

What happened is you tried it, and one of the few things that *always* goes wrong did its thing and went wrong. So, a more useful response would be, "Hey, it's business as usual. Let's figure out which of these things it is and fix it."

Even when it's all working well, you want to continually monitor, test, and improve the performance of each step. A mindset of continuous improvement is key to becoming a great lean marketer. You must constantly experiment with variables like copy, design, and offers and look for ways to outperform your baseline.

In God We Trust. All Others Must Bring Data.

To determine exactly what is or isn't working, you need data. Without data, you're just another idiot with an opinion. As a lean marketer, you'll spend a lot of time looking at metrics.

You can break metrics up into two classes—leading metrics and lagging metrics.

Lagging metrics are historical and are what most people think of when it comes to metrics. They're things like profit, churn rate, sales revenue, and so on.

There's nothing much you can do about last month's numbers. Of course you should know them, but they're often a bit like the belated "careful there" you hear after you've just bumped your head—too little, too late. Without the situational awareness of leading metrics, you're "cruisin' for a bruisin'" and will end up with a headache.

Leading metrics are early warning mechanisms that allow you to course-correct before your business is negatively impacted. These leading metrics will differ by business or industry. For example, you may run an online business and make money by turning email subscribers into customers. You normally get an average of 100 email opt-ins per day from your website, but the number has plummeted for the past few days. That would be an important leading indicator to pay attention to and rectify before it severely impacts your future revenue. Perhaps there's a technical issue with your website or CRM system. Or, if social media is an important source of leads and sub-scribers, maybe you've been shadow-banned or penalized somehow.

If your business has a physical location, you might track leading metrics like appointment bookings or walk-in traffic.

Whether your leading metrics are trending up or down, you want to determine why and take appropriate action.

If your leading metrics are trending up, this awareness will allow you to double down on whatever's working and take advantage of opportunities that present themselves. For example, someone with a large following may have mentioned you or recommended your product. You want to strike while the iron is hot. If you wait for the numbers to appear on next month's financial statements and then try working backward, it'll be too late to do anything useful.

The Metric That Matters

There are all sorts of metrics you can (and should) measure, and we'll cover a few of them shortly, but there's one that stands above them all: lifetime value (LTV). LTV is how much you make from a customer over their entire tenure with you.

There are literally only two ways to grow your business:

1   Get more customers.
2   Make more money from existing customers.

Everyone understands getting more customers, and a lot of our marketing is focused on that. But less well understood are the huge compounding effects of increasing LTV.

Your LTV determines how much you can spend to acquire a cus-tomer, how much you can spend to delight and retain them, and how big of a moat you can create to keep competitors away.

A common mistake when calculating LTV is using revenue fig-ures rather than profit. This causes you to overvalue your customers. Overstating your LTV will lead you to believe you can spend far more to acquire them than is sustainable.

The exceptions to this are (typically venture-backed) businesses that are solely focused on growth and market penetration. In that case, revenue-based LTV calculations may make sense.

Here's a simple example of how to calculate profit-based LTV. For instance, if your customers spend an average of $1,000 per year and you incur $300 yearly in variable expenses related to these sales, the profit per year is $700. If your customers stay with you for three years on average, their lifetime value would be $2,100.

Your variable expenses include the cost of goods sold and the cost of performing the service. You might also include other variable costs that can be directly attributed to the sale, like credit card processing fees. Fixed expenses like rent, back office, and administration should be excluded from your LTV calculation.

You should regularly recalculate the average time customers stay with you, how much they spend, and how much it costs you to deliver, as these continuously change. Obviously, you want to increase average tenure and the amount the customer spends while variable costs remain stable or drop. Not all customers are equal, so it makes sense to calculate LTV for each of your major customer segments.

There are many ways to increase your LTV, including:

- Increasing prices

- Upselling additional complementary products or services

- Ascending customers to higher or more premium tiers of your product or service

- Increasing the frequency of purchase

- Reactivating lost or churned customers

LTV is something you need to spend a huge amount of time and energy thinking about. It should dominate your thoughts so much that if I woke you up at 3 a.m., I'd find that you were dreaming about ways to increase it. LTV is your path to exponential growth.

Customer Acquisition Cost

Closely related to LTV is customer acquisition cost (CAC). This represents the average cost to acquire a new customer. It includes costs like advertising and resources spent on marketing and sales efforts.

For example, if you spent $100,000 on marketing and sales and acquired 1,000 new customers, your CAC would be $100.

All other things being equal (and they never are), whoever can afford to spend the most to acquire and retain a customer will win. That's one of the reasons LTV is so critical. If your LTV is low, you'll try to scrimp and save when acquiring and retaining customers. This rarely leads to amazing customer experiences.

In the absence of resources, you'll need to be resourceful. Scrappy, outside-the-box thinking is a specialty of founders and entrepreneurs. This is great at first, but increasing your LTV should be your biggest priority so that you can sustainably grow and scale.

Measuring the Returns

Return on ad spend (ROAS) and return on investment (ROI) are important metrics for measuring the success of your marketing and advertising.

ROAS is the *revenue* generated by an ad campaign divided by the cost of running it. ROI is the total *profit* generated divided by what it cost.

ROAS is generally a more granular metric that can be used to compare the performance of different campaigns, ad sets, or platforms. It's typically used for performance-based marketing campaigns, such as those using pay-per-click advertising.

ROI is a broader metric that can be used to understand the overall profitability of a strategy or media channel. It's the metric that essentially tells you if what you're doing is worth the investment.

Subscription Metrics

If you have a subscription model or offering in your business, two important metrics to track are monthly recurring revenue (MRR) and churn rate.

It would be awesome if every subscription customer we acquired stayed with us forever, but that's rarely the case. If you have a subscription-based offering, you need to measure attrition. Your churn rate is the percentage of customers who stop using your service during a given timeframe, typically monthly.

Think of MRR like water in your bucket. The water represents your predictable revenue at the start of the month. The churn rate is how fast your bucket leaks. You need to top up the bucket faster than it's leaking.

For example, if you have 1,000 subscribers paying $10 per month, your MRR would be $10,000. If you have a 2 percent monthly churn rate, you're losing 20 customers per month. This means your sales and marketing efforts need to acquire 20 customers every month just to maintain the status quo and more than that to actually grow.

High churn can signal customer dissatisfaction, lack of perceived value, or other potential business challenges.

Micrometrics

More fiction gets written in spreadsheets than in books. If you pluck the right arbitrary metrics and use them in isolation, you can make any campaign look good—and many marketers do just that.

The following are what I call micrometrics. In isolation, they don't mean much, but they can help you drill down into individual elements of your campaign, which can be extremely useful when troubleshooting.

Conversion Rate: The percentage of visitors who take a desired action, whether that's buying a product, opting in to your email list, or any other conversion goal.

Click-Through Rate (CTR): For digital ads, this metric represents the percentage of people who clicked on the ad after seeing it.

Cost Per Click (CPC): The average amount paid for each click in a pay-per-click advertising campaign.

Traffic: The number of visitors to your website or a specific page. This can be measured by unique visitors or page views.

Bounce Rate: The percentage of visitors who leave your website after viewing only one page.

Engagement Rate: On social platforms, this measures interactions on a post or campaign, such as likes, shares, and comments.

Lead-to-Customer Rate: How many potential customers convert into actual customers.

Marketing Qualified Lead (MQL): A lead deemed more likely to become a customer based on their engagement with marketing initiatives but isn't yet ready for a direct sales approach.

Sales Qualified Lead (SQL): A lead that has been qualified further, met specific criteria, and is considered ready to engage with sales.

Net Promoter Score (NPS): Measures customer loyalty and satisfaction. Customers are asked how likely they are to recommend a business on a scale from 0 to 10. Customers who rate their likelihood as 9 or 10 are classified as Promoters. Those who rate it as 7 or 8 are Passives, and those who rate between 0 and 6 are Detractors. The NPS is calculated by subtracting the percentage of Detractors from the percentage of Promoters, resulting in a score ranging from -100 to 100.

Email Open and Click Rates: For email marketing, these metrics track how many recipients open an email and how many click on the links within it.

Average Order Value (AOV): The average amount a customer spends in a single transaction.

Products Per Customer: The average number of products each customer has purchased.

Know the Numbers

James Clear wrote, "The two skills of modern business: Storytelling and spreadsheets. Know the numbers. Craft the narrative." I totally agree.

It's easy to be overwhelmed by the volume and scope of all the possible metrics you can track. I recommend creating a dashboard with the handful that are most impactful to your business and specific situation. Then, watch them closely and regularly. When you need to troubleshoot, which will be often, you can expand your scope.

The last thing to be mindful of when looking at your metrics is the time horizon. In the same way that handpicked individual metrics can obfuscate the truth, so can the time horizon in which you look at your metrics.

Shifting your perspective to the long term is like zooming out on a map. It allows you to see contours that you couldn't see before. This zoomed-out view is great for seeing larger trends but will lose important details. It will tell you that the average zebra is gray. You only see the black and white stripes when you zoom back in.

When making decisions, you must understand what the numbers tell you at both a macro and micro level. As a great marketer, you might be a lady (or gentleman) in the streets, but you'll be a freak in the spreadsheets. 😜

Chapter 15 Action Items

- Select the leading and lagging metrics that are most relevant to your business.

- Know and closely monitor your customer lifetime value and cost of customer acquisition.

- Create a metrics dashboard and watch it closely.

Conclusion

Be Dumb and Execute With Intensity

Over the years, marketing has become bloated. There are more things to do and more ways to do them. It's exhausting, ineffective, and wasteful.

My friend Dr. Ben Carvosso, a high-performance expert, recommends "compressing for quality." This means doing less stuff, being more intentional and focused, and, as a result, having more impact. Applying this to marketing is so refreshing. It's what lean marketing is all about.

But compressing for quality is not to be confused with the old "quality over quantity" cliché. Reps matter.

I've noticed a surprising pattern in my years of coaching, consulting, and mentoring. Guess what type of person wins most often? Is it the best-resourced person? No. Is it the luckiest? That helps, but also no. Is it the smartest? Actually, the opposite. This was a very surprising discovery.

Often, smart people try to plan every detail to perfection and either never execute or execute with a low level of intensity. They hate failing and looking stupid, which is a big problem because these will be recurring themes in your life as an entrepreneur and marketer.

For this reason, I urge you to "be dumb" and execute with intensity. Creating high-quality output is preceded by doing it poorly lots of times but continuously improving. Every master was once a disaster.

You've been equipped to win the game of marketing. Use the three force multipliers to give yourself leverage and massively amplify your results. Implement the nine principles of lean marketing and become a top 1 percent marketer. While your competitors are interrupting, shouting, and flailing about with random acts of marketing, you'll stand out because of your lean, intentional, and value-driven approach. It'll feel like bringing a gun to a knife fight.

Lastly, I urge you to get started immediately. Inspiration is highly perishable. The time to act is when the idea is hot, and the emotion around it is strong. "I do" beats IQ every time. So, take one impactful idea you learned from this book and make some progress on it *today*. Don't just nod your head at that. Really, get started *right now*.

There's So Much More

At a certain length, any nonfiction book becomes cumbersome. There's a balancing act every author must make between completeness and tedium. I don't want to be that guest who overstays their welcome, and I hope I haven't been.

Marketing is an expansive topic, and editing is a brutal business. Much of what I wrote for this book has ended up on the cutting-room floor. I agonized about each cut—powerful chapters, valuable concepts, and practical tactics. What's left is what some musicians call an "essentials" album—the most important pieces for most people. However, those who dig deeper into the B-sides and lesser-known tracks are richly rewarded.

If you're that way inclined, I have much more for you inside the Lean Marketing Hub. There, you can freely access resources that go beyond the book, ask questions, and take your journey into lean marketing further.

Importantly, it's a safe space for entrepreneurs. The isolation of being an entrepreneur is both unexpected and dangerous. It's dangerous because the absence of a peer group can decrease motivation, lead to poor decision-making, and result in burnout. It's also dangerous because there's a lack of qualified sounding boards. Proximity to peers on a similar journey and mentors is vital.

As an entrepreneur, you often feel like a lost tour guide who can't be seen scrutinizing a map in front of your group of paying holidaymakers. When customers, investors, or even family ask how it's going, you say, "It's going great! We're crushing it," when often the truth is it's crushing *you*.

Being part of a community of like-minded people who understand entrepreneurship can make the journey less lonely and hazardous. We're all solving similar problems and are on a similar path.

Join us for free at LeanMarketing.com/hub

Pay It Forward

I've always felt uneasy when entrepreneurs and successful people say they're "giving back."

Giving back suggests that you took too much, but that's not the game we entrepreneurs play.

We create value in the marketplace and then capture a small portion of it for ourselves. That way, our customers, our communities, and indeed the world always get the better deal. That's fair, that's sustainable, and frankly, it's fun.

That's what I've tried to do with this book. I've given you my best stuff and held nothing back. I've put more time, money, energy, and myself into it than I could ever reasonably justify.

Instead of "giving back," which implies a debt, I prefer "paying it forward," which implies generosity.

If you believe I've accomplished my goal with this book and given you value, I'd ask you to consider paying it forward by sharing it with someone who may benefit from it.

I've received such generosity many times when a mentor, friend, or colleague saw me struggling with something or sensed some untapped potential in me. They changed my life by saying, "Here, read this book." Who could you do that for?

Another way to pay it forward would be to leave a review. This helps others discover this book.

About the Author

Hey, thanks for reading.

This is the bit where I'm supposed to tell you how awesome I am. It's also usually written in the third person, which is kind of weird, so I won't do that.

I think people read "about" pages and author bios for two main reasons. They want to know, "Is this person credible?" and "What can they do for me?" With that in mind, here's a bunch of business stuff I've done that I'm proud of:

- I've sold a lot of books. I'm in the top 0.01 percent of nonfiction authors.

- My books have a lot of reach. They've been translated into over 30 languages and have impacted millions of entrepreneurs all over the world.

- I've founded, scaled, and successfully exited multiple high-growth businesses across various industries, including IT, telecommunications, and marketing.

- I've spoken to thousands of people at some amazing events and conferences.

- I've made a lot of money along the way. I know money doesn't buy happiness, but having grown up poor, I can tell you being rich is much better.

- I work very reasonable hours. My business and work support my lifestyle, health, and relationships rather than being detrimental to them.

Here's what I can do for you:

- I'll give you a clear, simple, and structured framework for marketing success.

- I'll help you and your team build your marketing skills, infrastructure, and capabilities.

- I'll help you grow your business revenue and profit.

- I'll help you increase the value of your business and create an asset that's salable, should you ever decide you want to exit.

- I'll help you build the kind of business that allows you to live life on your own terms.

- We'll do all of the above in a way that's fun.

You can contact me via email at **allan@LeanMarketing.com**—I love hearing from readers.